AFFILIATE MARKETING MASTERY

NICHOLAS DAVIS

AFFILIATE MARKETING MASTERY

NICHOLAS DAVIS

Welcome to Affiliate Marketing Mastery! In this ebook, we will delve into the world of affiliate marketing and show you how to build a profitable online business that generates passive income. Whether you're a seasoned marketer or a beginner, this guide will provide you with valuable insights and strategies to maximize your affiliate marketing success.

- Understanding Affiliate Marketing:

Affiliate marketing has emerged as a powerful and dynamic online business model that has the potential to revolutionize your life. With the growth of e-commerce and the digital economy, affiliate marketing offers individuals the opportunity to generate passive income and achieve financial independence. In this chapter, we will delve into a detailed understanding of affiliate marketing and explore how it can be leveraged to enhance your life.

1. What is Affiliate Marketing?
Affiliate marketing is a performance-based marketing strategy in which individuals

(affiliates) promote products or services of a company (merchant) and earn a commission for every successful sale or action generated through their marketing efforts. It is a win-win situation where affiliates earn money by driving valuable customers to the merchant's website, and the merchant benefits from increased sales and brand exposure.

2. How Does Affiliate Marketing Work?
The affiliate marketing process typically involves the following key players:

a) Merchant: The merchant is the product or service owner who is willing to pay a commission to affiliates for promoting their offerings. Merchants can be businesses, online retailers, or even individuals with digital products.

b) Affiliate: Affiliates are individuals or website owners who sign up for an affiliate program to promote the merchant's products. They utilize various marketing channels, such as websites, blogs, social media, email marketing, or video platforms, to attract potential customers.

c) Consumer: Consumers are the target audience who visit the affiliate's marketing channels and are interested in purchasing the merchant's products or services. The affiliate's goal is to convince and guide consumers to make a purchase through their unique affiliate link or coupon code.

d) Affiliate Network/Platform: In many cases, affiliate programs are facilitated by affiliate networks or platforms. These platforms act as intermediaries, providing a centralized hub where merchants and affiliates can connect, track sales, and manage commissions.

3. Benefits of Affiliate Marketing: Understanding the benefits of affiliate marketing is crucial for realizing its potential impact on your life. Here are some key advantages:

a) Passive Income: Affiliate marketing allows you to earn passive income. Once you have set up your marketing channels and established an audience, your efforts can generate income even while you sleep.

b) Flexibility and Freedom: As an affiliate marketer, you have the freedom to work from anywhere and at any time. You are not bound by traditional employment structures and can design your own schedule.

c) Low Startup Costs: Compared to other business models, affiliate marketing requires minimal upfront investment. You don't need to create your own products, manage inventory, or handle customer support. Instead, you focus on promoting existing products and earning commissions.

d) Diverse Revenue Streams: Affiliate marketing provides opportunities to diversify your income streams by promoting multiple products from different merchants. This helps mitigate risks and increases your earning potential.

e) Scalability: As your affiliate marketing efforts grow, you can scale your business by expanding your reach, targeting new markets, or exploring additional affiliate programs. The potential for growth is virtually limitless.

4. Building a Successful Affiliate Marketing Business:
To better your life through affiliate marketing, it is important to adopt effective strategies and best practices. Here are some key steps to build a successful affiliate marketing business:

a) Choose Your Niche: Select a niche that aligns with your interests, knowledge, and target audience. Focusing on a specific niche allows you to establish yourself as an authority and effectively cater to your audience's needs.

b) Research and Select Affiliate Programs: Conduct thorough research to find reputable affiliate programs with high-quality products or services that resonate with your niche. Evaluate their commission structures, track records, and affiliate support.

c) Build Your Online Presence: Establish a strong online presence through a website, blog, or social media platforms. Create valuable content, such as product reviews, tutorials, or informative articles, to attract and engage your audience.

d) Drive Targeted Traffic: Utilize various marketing techniques to drive targeted traffic to your affiliate links, such as search engine optimization (SEO), social media marketing, email marketing, or paid advertising. Focus on providing value and solving your audience's problems.

e) Monitor and Optimize: Regularly monitor your affiliate marketing performance, analyze data, and optimize your strategies accordingly. Experiment with different promotional methods, track conversions, and refine your approach to maximize your earnings.

Conclusion:
Affiliate marketing offers a transformative opportunity to generate passive income, achieve financial freedom, and design a lifestyle that suits your aspirations. By understanding the core concepts and implementing effective strategies, you can harness the power of affiliate marketing to better your life and unlock new possibilities for personal and professional growth.

The role of affiliates, merchants, and consumers in the affiliate market process

The success of affiliate marketing relies on the collaboration between three key players: affiliates, merchants, and consumers. Each participant plays a crucial role in driving the affiliate marketing process forward. In this chapter, we will explore the distinct roles and responsibilities of affiliates, merchants, and consumers, highlighting their contributions and interactions within the affiliate marketing ecosystem.

1. Affiliates:
Affiliates are the driving force behind affiliate marketing. They act as intermediaries between merchants and consumers, utilizing their marketing skills and online platforms to promote products or services. Here's a closer look at the role of affiliates:

a) Promoters and Marketers: Affiliates leverage various marketing channels, such as websites, blogs, social media platforms, email lists, or video channels, to promote the products or services of merchants. They create compelling content, reviews, tutorials, or advertisements to attract the attention and interest of potential consumers.

b) Audience Builders: Affiliates focus on building and nurturing their audience within a specific niche. By providing valuable and relevant content, they establish themselves as trusted authorities and influencers within their niche, ensuring that their recommendations carry weight and influence.

c) Traffic Generators: Affiliates employ marketing techniques such as search engine optimization (SEO), social media marketing, paid advertising, or email campaigns to drive targeted traffic to the merchant's website. They strategically place affiliate links or display banners to encourage consumers to visit the merchant's site and make a purchase.

d) Relationship Builders: Successful affiliates understand the importance of building relationships with their audience and merchants. They engage with their audience through comments, emails, or social media interactions, responding to inquiries, providing assistance, and establishing trust. Affiliates also collaborate closely with merchants to optimize their marketing efforts and negotiate better commission rates or exclusive deals.

2. Merchants:
Merchants are the product or service owners who collaborate with affiliates to expand their reach and increase sales. They provide affiliates with marketing materials, tracking systems, and commission structures. Let's explore the role of merchants:

a) Product or Service Providers: Merchants develop and offer products or services that align with their target market. They rely on affiliates to market and promote these offerings to a broader audience, driving traffic and generating sales.

b) Affiliate Program Managers: Merchants manage their affiliate programs, providing affiliates with access to marketing materials, affiliate links, and tracking systems. They monitor affiliate performance, track conversions, and ensure timely commission payments.

c) Commission Setters: Merchants determine the commission structure and payout rates for their affiliates. These can be based on a percentage of sales, a fixed amount per action (such as lead generation or app download), or a combination of both.

d) Relationship Managers: Merchants establish and maintain relationships with affiliates to ensure effective collaboration. They may offer additional incentives, exclusive deals, or support to high-performing affiliates to encourage continued promotion.

3. Consumers:
Consumers are the target audience of both affiliates and merchants. Their role is crucial in completing the affiliate marketing cycle. Here's how consumers contribute to the process:

a) Targeted Audience: Consumers are attracted to the content and recommendations provided by affiliates within their niche. They actively seek information, advice, or reviews to make informed purchase decisions.

b) Purchasers: Consumers visit the affiliate's marketing channels, click on affiliate links or use affiliate-provided coupon codes, and make purchases on the merchant's website. This transaction completes the conversion process, resulting in a commission for the affiliate.

c) Feedback Providers: Consumers may provide valuable feedback, reviews, or testimonials about the products or services they purchased. This feedback can be used by affiliates to further enhance their marketing strategies and by merchants to improve their offerings.

d) Repeat Customers: Satisfied consumers who have had a positive experience may become repeat customers, making additional purchases through the affiliate's links or directly from the merchant. This recurring business benefits both affiliates and merchants.

Conclusion:

Affiliate marketing thrives on the collaboration and synergy among affiliates, merchants, and consumers. Affiliates play a pivotal role in promoting products or services, merchants provide the offerings and infrastructure, and consumers complete the transaction process. Understanding the distinct roles of each participant and their interactions within the affiliate marketing process is essential for building successful and mutually beneficial partnerships.

• Exploring the benefits and potential income streams of affiliate marketing.

Affiliate marketing has gained significant traction as a viable online business model, offering individuals the opportunity to generate income and build a sustainable online presence. In this chapter, we will delve into the benefits of affiliate marketing and explore the various income streams it presents. Understanding these advantages and potential earnings will provide you with the foundation to maximize the potential of affiliate marketing.

1. Benefits of Affiliate Marketing:
Affiliate marketing offers several benefits that make it an attractive venture for individuals seeking financial independence and flexible work arrangements. Here are some key advantages:

a) Passive Income: One of the most significant benefits of affiliate marketing is the potential to earn passive income. Once you have established your affiliate marketing channels and implemented effective strategies, your efforts can continue to generate income even when you're not actively promoting products.

b) Low Startup Costs: Compared to traditional businesses, affiliate marketing has low startup costs. You don't need to create your own products or invest in inventory, making it an accessible option for aspiring entrepreneurs. Additionally, many affiliate programs are free to join, eliminating any upfront fees.

c) Flexibility and Freedom: Affiliate marketing allows you to work on your own terms. You have the freedom to choose the products or services you want to promote, set your own schedule, and work from anywhere with an internet connection. This flexibility enables you to create a work-life balance that suits your lifestyle.

d) No Customer Support or Inventory Management: As an affiliate marketer, you don't have to worry about customer support, product fulfillment, or inventory management. These responsibilities lie with the merchant. Your primary focus is on marketing and driving traffic to the merchant's products, leaving the operational aspects to the merchant.

e) Diverse Range of Products and Niches: Affiliate marketing offers a vast array of products and niches to choose from. You can align your promotions with your personal interests or expertise, allowing you to genuinely engage with your audience and provide valuable recommendations. The diversity of options ensures that you can find products that resonate with your target market.

2. Potential Income Streams in Affiliate Marketing:
Affiliate marketing presents various income streams that can contribute to your overall earnings. Here are some common avenues to explore:

a) Pay-Per-Sale (PPS): This is the most prevalent commission structure in affiliate marketing. Affiliates earn a percentage of the sale value when a customer referred by the affiliate makes a purchase. The commission rate varies across affiliate programs and products.

b) Pay-Per-Lead (PPL): Some affiliate programs pay commissions based on lead generation. Affiliates earn a predetermined amount when a referred customer takes a specific action, such as signing up for a newsletter, completing a form, or downloading an app.

c) Pay-Per-Click (PPC): Pay-per-click affiliate programs reward affiliates for driving traffic to the merchant's website. Affiliates earn a commission for each click their referral generates, regardless of whether a purchase is made. However, PPC programs tend to offer lower commission rates compared to PPS or PPL models.

d) Recurring Commissions: Some affiliate programs offer recurring commissions for subscription-based products or services. As long as the referred customer remains subscribed, affiliates earn commissions on a recurring basis. This can provide a steady and predictable income stream over time.

e) Two-Tier Programs: Two-tier affiliate programs allow affiliates to earn commissions not only from their own direct referrals but also from the affiliates they recruit. Affiliates receive a portion of the commissions generated by their recruited affiliates, providing an additional income stream.

f) Product Reviews and Recommendations: Affiliates can monetize their content by writing product reviews, creating comparison guides, or making recommendations to their audience. By leveraging their expertise and influencing their followers' purchasing decisions, affiliates can earn commissions when their recommendations result in sales.

g) Sponsored Content and Partnerships: Established affiliates with a sizable audience can collaborate with merchants on sponsored content or partnerships. Merchants may provide additional compensation or exclusive offers to affiliates in exchange for enhanced exposure or promotional activities.

Conclusion:

Affiliate marketing offers a range of benefits and income streams that can significantly impact your financial well-being and lifestyle. The potential for passive income, low startup costs, flexibility, and diverse product options make it an attractive venture. By understanding the advantages of affiliate marketing and exploring the various income streams available, you can build a successful and rewarding affiliate marketing business that aligns with your goals and aspirations.

● The importance of choosing the right niche for your affiliate marketing venture.

Choosing the right niche is a critical factor in the success of your affiliate marketing venture. A niche defines your target audience, the products you promote, and the overall direction of your marketing efforts. In this chapter, we will explore the importance of selecting the right niche and how it can significantly impact the effectiveness and profitability of your affiliate marketing business.

1. Understanding Niche Selection:
A niche is a specialized segment of a broader market. It focuses on a specific interest, demographic, or problem that a target audience faces. Here's why selecting the right niche is crucial for your affiliate marketing venture:

a) Audience Relevance: Choosing a niche that aligns with your audience's interests and needs is essential. By catering to a specific audience, you can provide valuable content, establish credibility, and develop a loyal following.

Targeted marketing efforts yield better results compared to a generic approach.

b) Authority and Expertise: When you choose a niche that you are passionate about or have expertise in, you position yourself as an authority in that area. Your knowledge and enthusiasm shine through your content, earning the trust and respect of your audience. This credibility enhances your ability to influence purchasing decisions and generate conversions.

c) Reduced Competition: Focusing on a specific niche allows you to differentiate yourself from broader competitors. By narrowing your target market, you face less competition and can establish a unique selling proposition. This increases your chances of standing out and capturing a dedicated audience.

d) Increased Conversion Rates: A well-defined niche allows you to tailor your marketing messages and recommendations to a specific audience. When your content speaks directly to their needs and desires, the likelihood of conversions and sales increases. Targeted marketing efforts result in higher conversion rates compared to a scattergun approach.

2. Researching and Evaluating Potential Niches:
To choose the right niche, it is crucial to conduct thorough research and evaluation. Consider the following factors when researching potential niches:

a) Passion and Interest: Start by identifying niches that align with your own passions, hobbies, or areas of interest. Affiliate marketing requires consistent effort, and having a genuine interest in your niche will keep you motivated and engaged in the long run.

b) Market Demand: Assess the market demand for your potential niches. Look for indications of a sizeable target audience, active communities, relevant forums, or social media engagement. High demand ensures a larger pool of potential customers to engage with and sell to.

c) Profitability: Evaluate the profit potential of your chosen niche. Research affiliate programs and products within the niche to ensure there are suitable options available with attractive commission structures. Consider the price range of products, the target audience's purchasing power, and the potential for upsells or recurring revenue.

d) Competition Analysis: Study the competition within the niche. Assess the number and quality of existing affiliates, the competitiveness of keywords and search rankings, and the overall saturation of the market. While competition can be a positive sign of a viable niche, it is essential to identify areas where you can differentiate yourself and add unique value.

e) Long-Term Viability: Consider the long-term viability and growth potential of your chosen niche. Look for emerging trends, technological advancements, or evolving consumer demands that may shape the future of the niche. Choosing a niche with long-term sustainability ensures the longevity and scalability of your affiliate marketing venture.

marketing efforts result in higher conversion rates compared to a scattergun approach.

2. Researching and Evaluating Potential Niches:

To choose the right niche, it is crucial to conduct thorough research and evaluation. Consider the following factors when researching potential niches:

a) Passion and Interest: Start by identifying niches that align with your own passions, hobbies, or areas of interest. Affiliate marketing requires consistent effort, and having a genuine interest in your niche will keep you motivated and engaged in the long run.

b) Market Demand: Assess the market demand for your potential niches. Look for indications of a sizeable target audience, active communities, relevant forums, or social media engagement. High demand ensures a larger pool of potential customers to engage with and sell to.

c) Profitability: Evaluate the profit potential of your chosen niche. Research affiliate programs and products within the niche to ensure there are suitable options available with attractive commission structures. Consider the price range of products, the target audience's purchasing power, and the potential for upsells or recurring revenue.

d) Competition Analysis: Study the competition within the niche. Assess the number and quality of existing affiliates, the competitiveness of keywords and search rankings, and the overall saturation of the market. While competition can be a positive sign of a viable niche, it is essential to identify areas where you can differentiate yourself and add unique value.

e) Long-Term Viability: Consider the long-term viability and growth potential of your chosen niche. Look for emerging trends, technological advancements, or evolving consumer demands that may shape the future of the niche. Choosing a niche with long-term sustainability ensures the longevity and scalability of your affiliate marketing venture.

3. Niche Expansion and Diversification:
As your affiliate marketing business grows, you may consider expanding or diversifying your niche portfolio. This can help you tap into new markets, reach a wider audience, and mitigate risks associated with relying heavily on a single niche. However, expansion should be strategic and align with your overall business goals to maintain focus and expertise.

Conclusion:
Choosing the right niche is a critical foundation for a successful affiliate marketing venture. By selecting a niche that aligns with your interests, has market demand, and offers profitability, you position yourself for success. Researching and evaluating potential niches, understanding the audience's needs, and staying committed to providing value will ensure the long-term viability and profitability of your affiliate marketing business.

- Conducting market research to identify profitable niches.

Market research plays a pivotal role in the process of identifying profitable niches for your affiliate marketing venture. It helps you understand market demand, consumer behavior, competition, and profit potential. In this chapter, we will explore the steps involved in conducting effective market research to identify profitable niches that align with your affiliate marketing goals.

1. Define Your Affiliate Marketing Goals:
Before diving into market research, it's essential to define your affiliate marketing goals. Consider factors such as your desired income level, target audience, interests, and long-term objectives. This clarity will guide your research and help you focus on niches that align with your goals.

2. Identify Potential Niches:
Start by brainstorming potential niches based on your interests, expertise, or areas of passion. Consider your hobbies, personal experiences,

professional background, or any emerging trends that catch your attention. Write down a list of potential niches to explore further.

3. Evaluate Market Demand:
Assessing market demand is crucial to determine the profitability of a niche. Here are key steps to evaluate market demand:

a) Keyword Research: Use keyword research tools like Google Keyword Planner, SEMrush, or Ubersuggest to identify keywords related to your potential niches. Look for high search volume and long-tail keywords that indicate active demand.

b) Competition Analysis: Study the competition within your potential niches. Analyze the number and quality of existing affiliates, the strength of their online presence, and the level of engagement in forums or social media communities. A healthy level of competition suggests market viability.

c) Trend Analysis: Monitor trends and emerging topics related to your potential niches. Google Trends, social media platforms, industry publications, and news sources can provide insights into the popularity and growth potential of a niche.

4. Assess Profit Potential:
Understanding the profit potential of a niche is essential for your affiliate marketing success. Consider the following factors:

a) Commission Structures: Research affiliate programs within your potential niches and analyze their commission structures. Look for programs that offer competitive commission rates, recurring commissions, or higher-priced products.

b) Product Availability: Evaluate the availability of relevant and high-quality products or services within your potential niches. Check if there are reputable merchants or affiliate networks that offer suitable products to promote.

c) Consumer Purchasing Power: Consider the purchasing power and willingness to spend within your target audience. Niches with affluent or passionate audiences may present higher profit potential as they are more likely to invest in products or services.

d) Upselling and Cross-selling Opportunities: Assess the potential for upselling or cross-selling within your niche. If there are complementary products or related services that can be promoted to the same audience, it can significantly increase your earning potential.

5. Validate Your Niche:
Once you have narrowed down your potential niches based on market demand and profit potential, it's crucial to validate your choices. Here are a few validation techniques:

a) Surveys and Interviews: Conduct surveys or interviews with your target audience to gather insights into their needs, pain points, and purchasing behaviors. This firsthand information can help you validate the viability of your chosen niches.

b) Social Media and Online Communities: Engage with online communities, forums, or social media groups relevant to your potential niches. Observe discussions, ask questions, and interact with the audience to gain deeper insights into their preferences and demands.

c) Pilot Testing: Consider piloting small-scale campaigns or content creation within your potential niches. Monitor engagement, conversion rates, and audience response to validate the viability of the niche before committing fully.

Conclusion:
Conducting thorough market research is a critical step in identifying profitable niches for your affiliate marketing venture. By evaluating market demand, assessing profit potential, and validating your chosen niches, you can make informed decisions that align with your affiliate marketing goals. Remember, market research is an ongoing process, and regularly staying updated with market trends and consumer preferences is key to maintaining a profitable affiliate marketing business.

Finding Profitable Affiliate Products:

Finding profitable affiliate products is a crucial step in building a successful affiliate marketing business. It involves researching and identifying products that resonate with your target audience, offer competitive commissions, and have the potential for high conversion rates. In this chapter, we will explore a comprehensive guide to help you find profitable affiliate products that align with your niche and maximize your earning potential.

1. Understand Your Target Audience:
Before diving into product research, it's essential to have a deep understanding of your target audience. Consider their demographics, interests, needs, and pain points. This understanding will guide your product selection process and enable you to offer solutions that genuinely resonate with your audience.

2. Research Affiliate Networks and Programs:

Affiliate networks and programs are valuable resources for finding profitable affiliate products. Here's how to navigate through them effectively:

a) Explore Major Affiliate Networks: Start by exploring reputable affiliate networks such as Amazon Associates, ShareASale, CJ Affiliate (formerly Commission Junction), and ClickBank. These networks provide a wide range of products across various niches.

b) Search for Niche-Specific Affiliate Programs: Look for affiliate programs that specifically cater to your niche. Conduct a Google search using keywords related to your niche, along with terms like "affiliate program" or "affiliate products." This can help you find programs that offer products specifically tailored to your audience.

c) Evaluate Commission Structures: Assess the commission structures offered by affiliate programs. Look for programs that provide competitive commission rates. Consider both percentage-based commissions and fixed commissions, depending on the product type and pricing.

d) Consider Affiliate Program Reputation: Research the reputation and track record of the affiliate programs you are considering. Look for reviews, testimonials, or feedback from other affiliates to ensure that the program is reliable, pays commissions on time, and provides adequate support and resources.

3. Analyze Product Demand and Popularity: Identifying products with high demand and popularity is crucial for profitability. Here are some effective strategies for analyzing product demand:

a) Keyword Research: Conduct keyword research using tools like Google Keyword Planner, SEMrush, or Ubersuggest to identify relevant keywords related to your niche and potential products. Look for keywords with high search volume and those indicating purchase intent.

b) Check Product Reviews and Ratings: Examine product reviews and ratings on e-commerce platforms, review websites, or social media. Positive reviews and high ratings indicate consumer satisfaction and potential demand for the product.

c) Study Trends and Seasonality: Monitor trends within your niche and identify products that align with emerging trends or seasonal demands. This can help you capitalize on current market interests and ensure the long-term viability of the products you promote.

4. Consider Product Quality and Relevance: Promoting high-quality and relevant products is crucial for building trust with your audience. Consider the following factors when evaluating product quality and relevance:

a) Product Features and Benefits: Assess the features, benefits, and unique selling points of the products. Ensure that they align with your audience's needs and preferences. Look for products that provide genuine value and address specific pain points.

b) Brand Reputation: Research the reputation and credibility of the brand or merchant offering the product. A reputable brand adds credibility to your recommendations and increases the likelihood of conversions.

c) Product Price Range: Consider the price range of the products and their affordability for your target audience. Balancing competitive commission rates with products that are within the purchasing power of your audience is important for conversion rates.

5. Test and Monitor Performance:
Once you have selected affiliate products, it's crucial to continuously test and monitor their performance. Track key metrics such as click-through rates, conversion rates, and overall revenue generated. Experiment with different promotional strategies, optimize your content, and adapt based on the data and insights you gather.

Conclusion:

Finding profitable affiliate products requires thorough research, an understanding of your target audience, and a keen eye for product demand and relevance. By leveraging affiliate networks, conducting keyword research, analyzing product demand, and considering quality and relevance, you can identify products that have the potential to drive conversions and maximize your earning potential. Continuously test and monitor the performance of your chosen products to refine your strategies and ensure long-term profitability in your affiliate marketing business.

- Exploring different affiliate networks and platforms.

Affiliate networks and platforms serve as essential intermediaries between affiliates and merchants, connecting them and facilitating the affiliate marketing process. They provide a centralized hub where affiliates can discover and join various affiliate programs, access marketing materials, track performance, and receive commission payments. In this chapter, we will explore different affiliate networks and platforms, highlighting their features, benefits, and notable examples to help you navigate the affiliate marketing landscape.

1. Amazon Associates:
Amazon Associates is one of the most popular and widely used affiliate networks, offering a vast range of products across numerous categories. Key features of Amazon Associates include:

a) Product Diversity: With millions of products available on Amazon, affiliates have the flexibility to promote a wide array of products within their niche.

b) Trusted Brand: Amazon is a well-established and reputable e-commerce platform, instilling trust and confidence in both affiliates and consumers.

c) Competitive Commissions: Amazon Associates offers commission rates ranging from 1% to 10%, depending on the product category and sales volume.

d) Advanced Tracking and Reporting: The platform provides robust tracking and reporting tools, allowing affiliates to monitor their performance, track clicks, conversions, and earnings.

2. ShareASale:
ShareASale is a popular affiliate network known for its extensive merchant base and diverse product offerings. Key features of ShareASale include:

a) Merchant Variety: ShareASale partners with thousands of merchants across various industries, providing affiliates with a wide range of products and niches to choose from.

b) Transparent Metrics: The network provides detailed performance metrics, allowing affiliates to monitor their clicks, conversions, earnings, and track the performance of individual merchants.

c) Affiliate Tools and Resources: ShareASale offers a suite of tools and resources to support affiliates, including banner creation, deep linking options, and data feeds.

d) Timely Payments: ShareASale ensures timely and reliable commission payments, typically on a monthly basis, with multiple payment options available.

3. CJ Affiliate (formerly Commission Junction):
CJ Affiliate is a well-established affiliate network that boasts a large pool of reputable merchants and advanced tracking capabilities. Key features of CJ Affiliate include:

a) Extensive Merchant Base: CJ Affiliate partners with top brands and merchants across various industries, providing affiliates with access to high-quality products and well-known brands.

b) Deep Linking and Product Catalogs: CJ Affiliate offers deep linking capabilities, allowing affiliates to link directly to specific product pages. It also provides access to comprehensive product catalogs for seamless product integration.

c) Real-Time Tracking and Reporting: The platform offers real-time tracking and reporting, enabling affiliates to monitor their performance, optimize campaigns, and gain insights into consumer behavior.

d) Dedicated Affiliate Support: CJ Affiliate provides dedicated support to affiliates, assisting with account setup, program selection, and troubleshooting.

4. ClickBank:
ClickBank is a digital product marketplace known for its wide range of digital and

information-based products, including e-books, courses, and software. Key features of ClickBank include:

a) Digital Product Focus: ClickBank specializes in digital products, making it an ideal platform for affiliates targeting niches within the digital space.

b) High Commission Rates: ClickBank offers high commission rates, often ranging from 50% to 75%, providing significant earning potential for affiliates.

c) Affiliate Marketplace: ClickBank features a marketplace where affiliates can discover and promote products based on popularity, gravity (indicating sales performance), and commission rates.

d) Reliable Tracking and Payments: ClickBank ensures accurate tracking of sales and timely commission payments to affiliates.

5. Impact:
Impact (formerly Impact Radius) is an affiliate marketing platform that focuses on

performance marketing and offers advanced tracking and reporting capabilities. Key features of Impact include:

a) Global Reach: Impact has a global presence, connecting affiliates with merchants from around the world, making it suitable for affiliates targeting international markets.

b) Advanced Tracking and Attribution: Impact provides advanced tracking and attribution capabilities, allowing affiliates to measure the impact of their marketing efforts accurately.

c) Partnership Automation: The platform goes beyond traditional affiliate marketing, offering partnership automation features that facilitate influencer marketing, strategic partnerships, and more.

d) Data-driven Insights: Impact provides robust analytics and reporting tools, empowering affiliates to make data-driven decisions and optimize their campaigns effectively.

Conclusion:

Exploring different affiliate networks and platforms is crucial for affiliate marketers seeking profitable partnerships and access to a wide range of products and niches. From established networks like Amazon Associates, ShareASale, and CJ Affiliate to specialized platforms like ClickBank and Impact, each network or platform offers unique features, benefits, and merchant partnerships. By understanding the offerings of different networks and platforms, affiliates can make informed decisions and select the most suitable options to maximize their affiliate marketing success.

- Strategies for identifying high-converting and reputable affiliate products.

Identifying high-converting and reputable affiliate products is crucial for maximizing your affiliate marketing success. By promoting products that not only generate significant conversions but also maintain a strong reputation, you can build trust with your audience and increase your earning potential. In this chapter, we will explore effective strategies to help you identify affiliate products that have a track record of high conversions and a reputable standing in the market.

1. Research and Understand Your Target Audience:
To identify high-converting affiliate products, it is essential to have a deep understanding of your target audience. Consider their demographics, preferences, needs, and pain points. This understanding will guide your product selection process and help you choose products that resonate with your audience's desires and provide valuable solutions.

2. Analyze Product Popularity and Demand: Analyzing product popularity and demand is a crucial step in identifying high-converting affiliate products. Here are effective strategies for conducting this analysis:

a) Keyword Research: Use keyword research tools to identify keywords and search terms related to your niche and potential products. Look for keywords with high search volume, indicating strong consumer interest and demand.

b) Trend Analysis: Stay updated with current trends and emerging topics within your niche. Monitor industry news, social media platforms, and relevant publications to identify products that align with trending interests and demands.

c) Consumer Reviews and Ratings: Research consumer reviews and ratings for potential affiliate products. Positive reviews and high ratings indicate consumer satisfaction and validate the product's quality and desirability.

d) Social Media Listening: Engage in social media listening by monitoring conversations, comments, and discussions related to your niche and potential products. This will provide insights into consumer sentiment, preferences, and popular products.

3. Evaluate Product Quality and Reputation: Promoting reputable affiliate products builds trust with your audience and increases the likelihood of conversions. Consider the following strategies to assess product quality and reputation:

a) Research Brand and Merchant Reputation: Investigate the reputation and credibility of the brand or merchant offering the product. Look for established brands with a history of delivering high-quality products and maintaining a positive reputation among consumers.

b) Read Customer Testimonials and Case Studies: Seek out customer testimonials and case studies related to the product. Genuine testimonials and success stories from satisfied customers provide strong evidence of the product's effectiveness and quality.

c) Check Product Specifications and Features: Evaluate the product's specifications, features, and benefits to ensure they align with your audience's needs. Look for products that offer unique selling points, solve specific problems, or provide exceptional value to consumers.

d) Research Return and Refund Policies: Understand the return and refund policies associated with the affiliate products you are considering. Reputable products often have customer-friendly policies, ensuring customer satisfaction and minimizing the risk of negative experiences.

4. Consider Affiliate Program Reputation and Support:
In addition to evaluating the product itself, it's important to consider the reputation and support provided by the affiliate program. Consider the following strategies:

a) Research Affiliate Program Reviews and Ratings: Look for reviews and ratings of the affiliate program you are considering. Pay attention to factors such as payment reliability, affiliate support, and overall satisfaction among affiliates.

b) Assess Affiliate Program Resources and Tools: Evaluate the resources and tools offered by the affiliate program. Look for programs that provide comprehensive marketing materials, tracking systems, reporting tools, and dedicated affiliate support to help you optimize your marketing efforts.

c) Communicate with Affiliate Managers: Reach out to affiliate managers or program representatives to ask questions, clarify doubts, and gauge their responsiveness and willingness to support affiliates. Effective communication and support from the affiliate program can greatly enhance your affiliate marketing experience.

Conclusion:

Identifying high-converting and reputable affiliate products requires diligent research and evaluation. By understanding your target audience, analyzing product popularity and demand, assessing product quality and reputation, and considering the reputation and support of the affiliate program, you can make informed decisions. Focus on promoting products that align with your audience's needs, have a strong reputation, and offer value, ultimately driving higher conversions and building a trustworthy affiliate marketing business.

- Evaluating commission structures, product relevance, and customer demand.

Evaluating commission structures, product relevance, and customer demand are essential steps in identifying profitable and successful affiliate products. By assessing these factors, you can ensure that the products you promote align with your target audience's needs, offer competitive commissions, and have a high potential for conversions. In this chapter, we will explore effective strategies for evaluating commission structures, product relevance, and customer demand to make informed decisions in your affiliate marketing endeavors.

1. Evaluating Commission Structures: Commission structures directly impact your earning potential as an affiliate marketer. Here are strategies to evaluate commission structures effectively:

a) Percentage-Based Commissions: Assess the commission rates offered by affiliate programs. Higher commission percentages can be advantageous, but consider the product price point and average sales volume. It's crucial to strike a balance between competitive commission rates and the actual revenue you can generate.

b) Fixed Commissions: Some affiliate programs offer fixed commissions per sale, lead, or action. Evaluate the fixed commission amounts and consider the overall profitability based on your audience's potential interest and the program's conversion rates.

c) Tiered Commission Structures: Some programs offer tiered commission structures, where your commission rate increases as you achieve higher sales volumes. Consider the potential for scaling your affiliate marketing business and earning higher commissions as you generate more sales.

d) Recurring Commissions: Explore affiliate programs that offer recurring commissions for subscription-based products or services. These programs can provide a steady and predictable income stream as long as the referred customers maintain their subscriptions.

2. Assessing Product Relevance:

Product relevance is crucial to engaging your target audience and driving conversions. Consider the following strategies to evaluate product relevance:

a) Audience Alignment: Analyze how well the product aligns with your target audience's interests, needs, and pain points. Determine if it addresses their specific challenges or offers solutions that are relevant to their lives.

b) Niche Compatibility: Ensure that the product fits within your chosen niche and complements your existing content or marketing strategies. Promoting products that resonate with your niche audience increases the likelihood of conversions.

c) Quality and Value: Evaluate the quality and value that the product offers to customers. Consider factors such as its features, benefits, pricing, customer support, and reputation. Choose products that provide genuine value and meet or exceed customer expectations.

d) Product Differentiation: Assess how the product stands out from competitors in terms of its unique selling points, innovation, or distinct features. Products with strong differentiators have a higher potential for success in the market.

3. Analyzing Customer Demand:
Analyzing customer demand ensures that you promote products that have a receptive market. Consider the following strategies to evaluate customer demand:

a) Keyword Research: Conduct keyword research to identify search volume and trends related to the product or its category. Look for keywords with high search volume and consistent or growing interest over time.

b) Market Research: Study market trends, industry reports, and consumer behavior within the niche to understand the demand for products. Identify emerging needs or changing preferences that can indicate potential customer demand.

c) Social Listening: Engage in social listening by monitoring conversations, comments, and discussions related to the product on social media platforms, forums, and review sites. Identify consumer sentiment, feedback, and overall demand for the product.

d) Customer Reviews and Ratings: Evaluate customer reviews and ratings for the product on e-commerce platforms or dedicated review websites. Positive reviews and high ratings indicate customer satisfaction and validate the demand for the product.

Conclusion:

Evaluating commission structures, product relevance, and customer demand is essential for selecting profitable and successful affiliate products. By considering the commission rates, product alignment with your target audience, and customer demand indicators such as keyword research, market analysis, social listening, and customer reviews, you can make informed decisions. Focus on promoting products that offer competitive commissions, align with your audience's needs, and have a demonstrated demand in the market. This strategic evaluation will maximize your chances of driving conversions and building a profitable affiliate marketing business.

Building a Captivating Affiliate Website:

Building a captivating affiliate website is essential for attracting and engaging your target audience, establishing credibility, and maximizing conversions. A well-designed and user-friendly website creates a positive user experience, encourages visitors to explore your content, and promotes the affiliate products you recommend. In this chapter, we will explore key strategies and best practices for building a captivating affiliate website that effectively drives traffic and generates revenue.

1. Define Your Website's Purpose and Niche: Clarify the purpose and focus of your affiliate website. Determine your niche and the specific audience you want to target. By defining your website's purpose and niche, you can tailor your content and design to meet the needs and interests of your target audience effectively.

2. Choose an Attractive and User-Friendly Design:
Select an attractive and user-friendly design that reflects your brand and appeals to your

target audience. Consider the following aspects:

a) Clean and Intuitive Layout: Opt for a clean and organized layout that makes it easy for visitors to navigate your website. Use intuitive menus, clear categories, and strategically placed call-to-action buttons.

b) Responsive Design: Ensure your website is responsive and mobile-friendly, as an increasing number of users access the internet via mobile devices. A responsive design ensures optimal viewing and usability across various screen sizes.

c) Visual Appeal: Use visually appealing elements such as high-quality images, graphics, and videos to enhance the visual appeal of your website. Balance the use of visuals with fast-loading times to maintain a smooth user experience.

3. Create Compelling and Relevant Content: Content is crucial for engaging your audience and driving conversions. Follow these

strategies to create compelling and relevant content:

a) High-Quality Blog Posts: Publish informative and engaging blog posts that provide value to your audience. Address their pain points, offer solutions, and include relevant affiliate product recommendations seamlessly within the content.

b) Product Reviews and Comparisons: Write in-depth and unbiased product reviews and comparisons to help your audience make informed purchasing decisions. Include personal experiences, pros and cons, and clear affiliate links to the recommended products.

c) How-To Guides and Tutorials: Offer step-by-step how-to guides and tutorials related to your niche and the products you promote. Help your audience understand product usage, offer tips, and demonstrate the benefits of the recommended products.

d) Engaging Visual Content: Incorporate visually appealing content such as infographics, videos, and interactive elements to enhance user engagement and convey information effectively.

4. Optimize Your Website for SEO:
Search engine optimization (SEO) is crucial for improving your website's visibility and attracting organic traffic. Implement the following SEO best practices:

a) Keyword Research: Conduct thorough keyword research to identify relevant keywords and phrases related to your niche. Incorporate these keywords naturally into your content, titles, meta descriptions, and image alt tags.

b) On-Page Optimization: Optimize your website's meta tags, headers, and URLs to align with your targeted keywords. Ensure your website structure is crawlable and well-organized, making it easy for search engines to understand and index your content.

c) Link Building: Implement a strategic link-building strategy to increase the authority and visibility of your website. Seek opportunities for guest blogging, collaborate with influencers, and earn backlinks from reputable websites in your niche.

d) Page Speed Optimization: Optimize your website's loading speed by compressing images, leveraging browser caching, and using a content delivery network (CDN). A fast-loading website improves user experience and search engine rankings.

5. Incorporate Clear Call-to-Actions:
Include clear and compelling call-to-action (CTA) buttons throughout your website to guide visitors towards your affiliate product recommendations. Use persuasive language and place CTAs strategically within your content, sidebar, and at the end of blog posts to encourage conversions.

6. Build Trust and Credibility:
Establishing trust and credibility is crucial for attracting and retaining visitors. Use the following strategies:

a) About Page: Create an informative and authentic "About" page that shares your story, expertise, and why visitors should trust your recommendations.

b) Testimonials and Social Proof: Include testimonials from satisfied customers, case studies, or social proof to showcase the positive experiences of others with the recommended products.

c) Transparent Affiliate Disclosure: Clearly disclose your affiliate relationships and ensure compliance with applicable disclosure guidelines. Transparency builds trust with your audience.

d) Authoritative Content: Consistently publish high-quality, well-researched content that positions you as an authority in your niche. Include credible sources, statistics, and expert opinions to enhance your credibility.

Conclusion:

Building a captivating affiliate website requires careful consideration of design, content, SEO optimization, and establishing trust with your audience. By defining your website's purpose, choosing an attractive design, creating compelling content, optimizing for SEO, incorporating clear CTAs, and building trust and credibility, you can create a captivating website that attracts visitors, engages them, and encourages conversions. Remember to regularly update and refine your website based on user feedback and industry trends to maintain its effectiveness and ensure long-term success in your affiliate marketing endeavors.

- Selecting a domain name and reliable hosting provider.

Selecting a domain name and choosing a reliable hosting provider are crucial steps in establishing a strong online presence for your affiliate marketing business. Your domain name represents your brand, while your hosting provider ensures the smooth functioning and accessibility of your website. In this chapter, we will explore key considerations and best practices to help you make informed decisions when selecting a domain name and a reliable hosting provider.

1. Selecting a Domain Name:
Your domain name is your website's address and plays a vital role in branding and user perception. Consider the following factors when selecting a domain name:

a) Brand Alignment: Choose a domain name that aligns with your brand, niche, or the focus of your affiliate marketing business. It should be memorable, relevant, and reflect your brand identity effectively.

b) Short and Easy to Remember: Opt for a domain name that is concise, easy to spell, and memorable. Avoid complex or hyphenated domain names that can confuse users and make it difficult for them to recall your website.

c) Keyword Inclusion: Consider incorporating relevant keywords into your domain name. This can help with search engine optimization (SEO) and convey the focus or niche of your website.

d) Domain Extension: Choose a domain extension that is appropriate for your business. While ".com" is the most common and widely recognized, other options such as ".net" or country-specific extensions like ".co.uk" may be suitable depending on your target audience and location.

e) Brand Protection: Consider registering variations of your domain name and relevant extensions to protect your brand from potential misuse or unauthorized use by others.

2. Choosing a Reliable Hosting Provider:
Your hosting provider is responsible for
ensuring your website is accessible, secure, and
operates smoothly. Consider the following
factors when selecting a reliable hosting
provider:

a) Uptime and Reliability: Choose a hosting
provider that guarantees high uptime, ideally
99% or higher. A reliable hosting provider
ensures your website remains accessible to
visitors, minimizing downtime and potential
revenue loss.

b) Speed and Performance: Opt for a hosting
provider that offers fast server response times
and excellent website loading speeds. A slow-
loading website can negatively impact user
experience and search engine rankings.

c) Scalability and Flexibility: Consider the
scalability and flexibility offered by the hosting
provider. Your website's traffic and resource
requirements may grow over time, so ensure
your hosting plan allows for easy scaling and

accommodates increased traffic without performance issues.

d) Customer Support: Select a hosting provider with responsive and knowledgeable customer support. This is crucial for troubleshooting technical issues, resolving concerns, and ensuring your website remains operational.

e) Security Measures: Ensure the hosting provider prioritizes website security, including features such as SSL certificates, regular backups, firewalls, and malware scanning. A secure hosting environment protects your website and the sensitive data of your visitors.

f) Cost and Value: Compare pricing plans and consider the value provided by the hosting provider. Look for plans that offer a balance between affordability and the features and resources required to support your website's needs.

3. Conducting Research and Comparisons: Before finalizing your domain name and hosting provider, conduct thorough research

and comparisons. Consider the following strategies:

a) Read Reviews and Recommendations: Explore reviews and recommendations from trusted sources, industry experts, and other website owners. Pay attention to feedback regarding reliability, customer support, uptime, and performance.

b) Seek Referrals and Feedback: Reach out to fellow affiliate marketers or website owners in relevant communities and seek their opinions and experiences with different domain registrars and hosting providers. Their insights can help you make informed decisions.

c) Check Hosting Features and Limitations: Review the hosting provider's features, such as storage, bandwidth, email accounts, and supported technologies. Ensure they align with your website's requirements and any future growth plans.

d) Consider Package Add-ons and Extras: Evaluate any additional services or extras provided by the hosting provider, such as-website builders, one-click installations, or marketing tools. These add-ons can enhance your website's functionality and ease of use.

Conclusion:
Selecting a domain name and a reliable hosting provider are critical steps in establishing and maintaining a successful affiliate marketing website. Choose a domain name that aligns with your brand, is easy to remember, and reflects your niche. When selecting a hosting provider, prioritize uptime, speed, scalability, customer support, security measures, and overall value. Conduct thorough research, read reviews, seek referrals, and compare options before making your final decisions. A well-chosen domain name and a reliable hosting provider lay the foundation for a smooth and impactful online presence, enabling you to focus on creating engaging content and driving conversions in your affiliate marketing journey.

- Designing an appealing and user-friendly website.

Designing an appealing and user-friendly website is crucial for engaging your audience, driving conversions, and establishing a strong online presence. A well-designed website enhances the user experience, communicates your brand effectively, and encourages visitors to explore your content and take desired actions. In this chapter, we will explore best practices and strategies for designing an appealing and user-friendly website that captivates your audience and maximizes your affiliate marketing success.

1. Plan Your Website Structure and Navigation: Before diving into the design process, plan your website's structure and navigation. Consider the following strategies:

a) Clear Hierarchy: Create a clear hierarchy with well-defined categories and subcategories. Organize your content in a logical and intuitive manner, making it easy for visitors to find what they are looking for.

b) Intuitive Menu: Use a clear and intuitive menu structure that allows visitors to navigate seamlessly through your website. Ensure the menu is prominently placed and easily accessible on all pages.

c) Breadcrumbs: Implement breadcrumbs to provide visitors with a clear path of their navigation and improve the overall user experience.

d) Search Functionality: Incorporate a search bar to allow visitors to quickly search for specific content or products within your website.

2. Choose an Attractive and Consistent Design: An appealing design enhances user engagement and reflects your brand identity. Consider the following design strategies:

a) Visual Consistency: Maintain a consistent visual style throughout your website. Use a cohesive color scheme, typography, and imagery that aligns with your brand and creates a harmonious user experience.

b) Use White Space: Utilize white space effectively to create a clean and uncluttered design. White space helps improve readability and draws attention to key elements on your website.

c) Attention-Grabbing Visuals: Incorporate high-quality images, graphics, and videos that are relevant to your content and resonate with your target audience. Visuals should support your message and enhance the overall aesthetic appeal of your website.

d) Responsive Design: Ensure your website is responsive and adapts seamlessly to various devices and screen sizes. A responsive design enhances the user experience and improves accessibility for mobile users.

3. Prioritize User-Friendly Navigation: User-friendly navigation is crucial for guiding visitors through your website. Consider the following navigation strategies:

a) Clear and Descriptive Labels: Use clear and descriptive labels for navigation menu items, buttons, and links. Visitors should easily understand where each link will lead them.

b) Sticky Navigation: Implement a sticky or fixed navigation bar that remains visible as visitors scroll through your website. This allows for easy access to the menu, enhancing navigation convenience.

c) Call-to-Action Placement: Strategically place call-to-action buttons and links to guide visitors towards desired actions, such as making a purchase or subscribing to a newsletter.

d) Internal Linking: Incorporate internal linking within your content to help visitors discover related articles or products. This encourages them to stay on your website longer and explore more of your content.

4. Optimize Page Loading Speed:
Fast page loading speed is crucial for a positive user experience. Consider the following strategies to optimize loading speed:

a) Image Optimization: Optimize images by compressing them without sacrificing quality. Use image formats that balance file size and visual quality, such as JPEG or PNG.

b) Minify Code: Minimize the size of your HTML, CSS, and JavaScript files by removing unnecessary spaces, comments, and line breaks. This reduces the loading time of your website.

c) Use Caching: Implement browser caching to store static resources on visitors' devices, reducing the need to retrieve them with each visit. Caching improves loading speed for returning visitors.

d) Content Delivery Network (CDN): Utilize a CDN to deliver your website's content from servers located closer to your visitors. This reduces latency and improves loading speed, especially for visitors from different geographic locations.

5. Prioritize Readability and Accessibility:

Ensure your website is readable and accessible to a wide range of users. Consider the following strategies:

a) Clear Typography: Use legible fonts, appropriate font sizes, and appropriate line spacing to enhance readability. Ensure there is sufficient contrast between the text and the background.

b) Accessibility Standards: Follow accessibility standards to ensure your website can be accessed and used by individuals with disabilities. This includes providing alt text for images, keyboard navigation support, and adherence to WCAG (Web Content Accessibility Guidelines) guidelines.

c) Break Content into Digestible Sections: Break up your content into smaller, easily scannable sections with headings, subheadings, and bullet points. This helps users quickly grasp the main points of your content.

d) Mobile-Friendly Design: Optimize your website for mobile devices by using responsive design techniques, ensuring content is easily accessible and readable on smaller screens.

Conclusion:

Designing an appealing and user-friendly website is crucial for maximizing engagement and conversions in your affiliate marketing efforts. By planning your website structure, choosing an attractive and consistent design, prioritizing user-friendly navigation, optimizing page loading speed, and ensuring readability and accessibility, you can create a captivating website that effectively communicates your brand, engages your audience, and drives affiliate marketing success. Regularly assess and refine your website based on user feedback and industry trends to ensure it remains appealing and user-friendly, adapting to the evolving needs of your visitors.

- Creating compelling content that engages and converts visitors.

Creating compelling content is a key element of successful affiliate marketing. Well-crafted content not only engages your audience but also persuades and convinces them to take desired actions, such as making a purchase or clicking on affiliate links. In this chapter, we will explore strategies and best practices for creating compelling content that captivates your visitors, builds trust, and maximizes conversions in your affiliate marketing endeavors.

1. Understand Your Target Audience:
Before creating content, it is essential to have a deep understanding of your target audience. Consider their demographics, interests, needs, pain points, and motivations. This understanding will help you tailor your content to resonate with your audience and address their specific challenges and desires.

2. Provide Valuable and Informative Content:

Create content that provides value and addresses the needs of your audience. Consider the following strategies:

a) Educational Articles and Guides: Publish informative articles, tutorials, and guides that offer practical tips, solutions, and insights. Position yourself as an authority in your niche by sharing valuable knowledge and expertise.

b) Product Reviews and Comparisons: Write in-depth and unbiased product reviews and comparisons. Provide honest evaluations, highlighting the benefits, features, and drawbacks of the products you are promoting. Include personal experiences, pros and cons, and clear affiliate links.

c) How-To Content: Create step-by-step how-to guides or tutorials that demonstrate how to use a product or solve a specific problem. Walk your audience through the process, offering practical advice and recommendations along the way.

d) Case Studies and Success Stories: Share real-life case studies and success stories related to the products or services you promote. Highlight the positive experiences and outcomes of actual customers, showcasing the benefits and results achieved.

3. Tell Engaging Stories:
Storytelling is a powerful technique that captivates and connects with your audience on an emotional level. Consider the following strategies:

a) Personal Anecdotes: Incorporate personal anecdotes and experiences to make your content relatable and authentic. Share stories that illustrate how a product or service has made a positive impact on your life or the lives of others.

b) Customer Testimonials: Include customer testimonials and success stories to add social proof and credibility to your content. Highlight how the product or service has helped customers overcome challenges and achieve desired outcomes.

c) Visual Storytelling: Use visual elements such as images, infographics, or videos to enhance your storytelling. Visuals can evoke emotions, simplify complex concepts, and engage your audience on a deeper level.

4. Utilize Persuasive Copywriting Techniques: Craft your content using persuasive copywriting techniques to influence and compel your audience. Consider the following strategies:

a) Clear and Compelling Headlines: Use attention-grabbing headlines that spark curiosity, convey the benefit or solution, and entice visitors to continue reading.

b) Benefits-Oriented Approach: Focus on highlighting the benefits and outcomes that your audience can achieve by using the products or services you promote. Emphasize how the products address their pain points or fulfill their desires.

c) Call-to-Action (CTA) Placement: Strategically place clear and persuasive calls-to-action (CTAs) throughout your content. Encourage visitors to take the desired action, such as clicking on affiliate links or making a purchase.

d) Use Emotional Triggers: Appeal to your audience's emotions by evoking feelings of desire, urgency, or empathy. Connect with their aspirations, fears, or desires to create a strong emotional connection and drive action.

5. Optimize for Search Engines:
To ensure your content reaches a wider audience, optimize it for search engines. Consider the following strategies:

a) Keyword Research: Conduct keyword research to identify relevant keywords and incorporate them naturally into your content. Optimize your headlines, subheadings, meta tags, and image alt tags.

b) Quality and Relevance: Create high-quality and relevant content that aligns with your targeted keywords. Search engines prioritize valuable and informative content that provides solutions to user queries.

c) Internal Linking: Incorporate internal links within your content to guide visitors to related articles or product recommendations. Internal linking improves the user experience and helps search engines discover and index your content.

d) Readability and Formatting: Ensure your content is easy to read and understand. Use proper formatting with clear headings, subheadings, bullet points, and paragraphs to enhance readability.

Conclusion:
Creating compelling content is crucial for engaging and converting your website visitors in affiliate marketing. By understanding your target audience, providing valuable content, storytelling, utilizing persuasive copywriting techniques, and optimizing for search engines, you can effectively captivate your audience, build trust, and drive conversions.-

Regularly assess and refine your content based on user feedback, data insights, and industry trends to ensure it remains compelling and relevant. Remember to balance promotional content with valuable information, maintaining the trust and interest of your audience.

- Optimizing your website for search engines (SEO) to drive organic traffic.

Optimizing your website for search engines is crucial for driving organic traffic and increasing visibility in search engine results. By implementing effective SEO strategies, you can improve your website's rankings, attract targeted visitors, and enhance the overall performance of your affiliate marketing efforts. In this chapter, we will explore key practices and strategies for optimizing your website for search engines and driving organic traffic to maximize your affiliate marketing success.

1. Keyword Research and Optimization: Keyword research forms the foundation of your SEO strategy. Consider the following strategies:

a) Identify Targeted Keywords: Research and identify relevant keywords and phrases that align with your niche and audience's search intent. Use keyword research tools to identify popular and low-competition keywords.

b) On-Page Optimization: Optimize your website's pages by incorporating targeted keywords naturally into key areas such as page titles, headings, meta descriptions, URL structures, and within the content itself.

c) Long-Tail Keywords: Target long-tail keywords, which are more specific and have lower competition. Long-tail keywords can help you attract highly targeted traffic and increase the likelihood of conversions.

d) Content Optimization: Create high-quality, informative, and valuable content that incorporates targeted keywords strategically. Aim to provide the best possible answer to users' queries, addressing their pain points and offering solutions.

2. Technical SEO Optimization:
Technical SEO focuses on improving your website's technical aspects for better search engine visibility. Consider the following strategies:

a) Website Speed: Optimize your website's loading speed by compressing images, enabling browser caching, minifying code, and utilizing a content delivery network (CDN).

b) Mobile-Friendliness: Ensure your website is mobile-friendly and provides a seamless user experience across various devices. Responsive design and mobile optimization are essential for ranking well in mobile search results.

c) Website Architecture: Create a logical and organized website structure that is easy to navigate. Use proper URL structures, clear hierarchy, and breadcrumbs to help search engines understand and index your website effectively.

d) XML Sitemap: Generate and submit an XML sitemap to search engines. A sitemap helps search engines crawl and index your website's pages more efficiently.

3. Quality Link Building:
Link building is an important aspect of off-page SEO and can improve your website's

authority and visibility. Consider the following strategies:

a) Guest Blogging: Contribute guest posts to reputable websites within your niche. This can help you build backlinks, drive referral traffic, and establish your expertise.

b) Influencer Outreach: Collaborate with influencers or industry experts to create valuable content and obtain backlinks from their websites or social media platforms.

c) Social Media Engagement: Actively engage with your audience on social media platforms, sharing your content and building relationships. Social signals and shares can indirectly influence your website's visibility.

d) Online Directories and Industry Associations: Submit your website to relevant online directories and industry associations. This can improve your website's visibility and provide valuable backlinks.

4. User Experience and Engagement:

Improving user experience and engagement signals can positively impact your website's SEO. Consider the following strategies:

a) Quality Content: Create valuable, informative, and engaging content that encourages visitors to spend more time on your website. This can reduce bounce rates and increase user engagement.

b) Internal Linking: Incorporate internal links within your content to guide visitors to related articles or product recommendations. Internal linking improves navigation and encourages users to explore more of your website.

c) User-Friendly Design: Ensure your website has a clean and intuitive design that is easy to navigate and visually appealing. A user-friendly design enhances user experience and encourages visitors to stay longer.

d) Reduce Page Load Times: Optimize your website's loading speed to provide a smooth and fast experience. Slow-loading websites can lead to higher bounce rates and negatively impact user experience.

5. Regular Monitoring and Optimization: SEO is an ongoing process that requires continuous monitoring and optimization. Consider the following strategies:

a) Monitor Website Analytics: Utilize tools like Google Analytics to track website metrics, user behavior, and keyword performance. Analyze the data to identify areas for improvement and optimization.

b) Content Updates: Regularly update and refresh your content to ensure it remains relevant and up-to-date. Consider adding new information, updating statistics, and optimizing for new keywords.

c) Monitor Keyword Rankings: Track your keyword rankings to identify opportunities and areas for improvement. Adjust your content and optimization strategies to enhance your rankings for targeted keywords.

d) Stay Up-to-Date with SEO Trends: Keep up with the latest SEO trends, algorithm updates, and best practices. Stay informed through industry blogs, forums, and reputable SEO resources.

Conclusion:

Optimizing your website for search engines is essential for driving organic traffic and maximizing your affiliate marketing success. By conducting thorough keyword research, optimizing your content and technical aspects, building quality backlinks, prioritizing user experience and engagement, and regularly monitoring and optimizing your SEO efforts, you can improve your website's visibility, attract targeted visitors, and increase conversions. Remember that SEO is an ongoing process, and staying up-to-date with the latest SEO trends and best practices will help you maintain a competitive edge in the evolving digital landscape.

Effective Marketing Strategies:

Effective marketing strategies are crucial for affiliate marketers to attract and engage their target audience, drive conversions, and maximize their affiliate marketing success. By implementing proven marketing strategies, you can promote your affiliate products effectively, build brand awareness, and establish long-lasting relationships with your audience. In this chapter, we will explore key marketing strategies that can help you achieve your affiliate marketing goals.

1. Content Marketing:
Content marketing is a powerful strategy for attracting and engaging your audience. Consider the following tactics:

a) Blogging: Create a blog where you can publish valuable and informative content related to your niche and the products you promote. Use SEO techniques to optimize your blog posts for search engines and incorporate affiliate links seamlessly.

b) Guest Posting: Contribute guest posts to reputable websites or blogs within your niche. This can help you reach a wider audience, build credibility, and drive referral traffic to your website.

c) Video Content: Create engaging video content such as product reviews, tutorials, or demonstrations. Leverage platforms like YouTube to showcase your expertise, build a loyal following, and incorporate affiliate links in video descriptions or annotations.

d) Email Marketing: Build an email list and develop a nurturing campaign to deliver valuable content, exclusive offers, and affiliate product recommendations to your subscribers. Use email automation tools to streamline your campaigns and track performance.

2. Social Media Marketing:
Social media platforms offer excellent opportunities to connect with your audience, build brand awareness, and drive traffic to your website. Consider the following strategies:

a) Platform Selection: Identify the social media platforms that align with your target audience. Focus on building a presence and engaging with your audience on platforms such as Facebook, Instagram, Twitter, or LinkedIn.

b) Consistent Branding: Maintain consistent branding across your social media profiles. Use high-quality visuals, compelling captions, and relevant hashtags to attract attention and build recognition.

c) Community Engagement: Actively engage with your audience by responding to comments, messages, and mentions. Encourage conversations, ask for feedback, and provide valuable insights to foster a sense of community.

d) Influencer Collaborations: Collaborate with influencers within your niche to expand your reach and tap into their engaged audience. Seek opportunities for sponsored posts, joint campaigns, or affiliate partnerships.

3. Search Engine Marketing (SEM):

Search engine marketing involves paid advertising to increase your website's visibility in search engine results. Consider the following tactics:

a) Pay-Per-Click (PPC) Advertising: Utilize platforms like Google Ads or Bing Ads to create targeted ad campaigns. Choose relevant keywords, create compelling ad copy, and drive traffic directly to your affiliate landing pages.

b) Display Advertising: Display ads on relevant websites or within ad networks to increase brand visibility and attract targeted visitors. Use appealing visuals and compelling ad copy to grab attention and generate clicks.

c) Remarketing: Implement remarketing campaigns to re-engage visitors who have previously shown interest in your website or products. Show targeted ads to these users across various platforms, reminding them of the products they were interested in.

4. Influencer Marketing:

Leverage the influence of popular individuals or industry experts to promote your affiliate products. Consider the following approaches:

a) Affiliate Partnerships: Collaborate with influencers and offer them an affiliate partnership. Provide them with unique affiliate links or discount codes to promote to their audience. This allows you to tap into their trust and credibility.

b) Sponsored Content: Sponsor influencer-created content, such as blog posts, videos, or social media posts that feature your affiliate products. Ensure the content aligns with your brand and resonates with the influencer's audience.

c) Giveaways and Contests: Organize giveaways or contests in collaboration with influencers. This can generate excitement, increase brand exposure, and attract new visitors to your website or social media channels.

5. Data Analytics and Tracking:

Utilize data analytics and tracking tools to monitor the performance of your marketing efforts. Consider the following strategies:

a) Conversion Tracking: Set up conversion tracking to measure the effectiveness of your affiliate links and marketing campaigns. Track metrics such as clicks, conversions, and revenue generated.

b) Google Analytics: Implement Google Analytics to gain insights into your website's performance, user behavior, and traffic sources. Analyze the data to identify trends, optimize your marketing strategies, and improve user experience.

c) A/B Testing: Conduct A/B testing to experiment with different marketing tactics, landing pages, or calls-to-action. Test variations to identify the most effective approaches and optimize for better results.

Conclusion:
Implementing effective marketing strategies is crucial for affiliate marketers to attract, engage, and convert their target audience. By-

leveraging content marketing, social media marketing, search engine marketing, influencer marketing, and utilizing data analytics and tracking tools, you can promote your affiliate products effectively and maximize your affiliate marketing success. Remember to consistently assess and refine your marketing strategies based on data insights, user feedback, and industry trends to stay ahead in the competitive affiliate marketing landscape.

- Implementing various marketing channels to promote your affiliate products.

Implementing diverse marketing channels is essential for affiliate marketers to reach a wider audience, drive traffic, and effectively promote their affiliate products. By leveraging different marketing channels, you can increase brand visibility, engage with your target audience, and maximize your affiliate marketing success. In this chapter, we will explore various marketing channels and strategies that you can utilize to promote your affiliate products effectively.

1. Content Marketing:
Content marketing involves creating and distributing valuable and informative content to attract and engage your audience. Consider the following content marketing strategies:

a) Blogging: Maintain a blog where you can publish high-quality articles, tutorials, and product reviews related to your niche.

Incorporate affiliate links seamlessly within your content to drive conversions.

b) Guest Posting: Contribute guest posts to reputable websites or blogs within your niche. This allows you to reach new audiences, build credibility, and drive referral traffic to your website.

c) Video Content: Create engaging video content on platforms like YouTube or social media channels. Produce product reviews, tutorials, or demonstrations that showcase the benefits and usage of your affiliate products. Include affiliate links in video descriptions or annotations.

d) Podcasting: Host a podcast where you discuss topics related to your niche, interview industry experts, or share valuable insights. Mention and promote your affiliate products during podcast episodes and include affiliate links in the episode descriptions.

2. Social Media Marketing:
Social media platforms provide a vast opportunity to connect with your audience,

build brand awareness, and promote your affiliate products. Consider the following social media marketing strategies:

a) Platform Selection: Identify the social media platforms that align with your target audience. Focus on building a presence and engaging with your audience on platforms such as Facebook, Instagram, Twitter, LinkedIn, or Pinterest.

b) Content Sharing: Regularly share valuable content, including blog posts, videos, product recommendations, or industry news, on your social media profiles. Use compelling visuals, compelling captions, and relevant hashtags to attract attention and drive engagement.

c) Influencer Collaborations: Collaborate with influencers or micro-influencers within your niche. Partner with them to promote your affiliate products through sponsored posts, reviews, or giveaways. Leverage their audience and credibility to expand your reach.

d) Social Media Advertising: Utilize paid social media advertising options to target specific demographics and increase your reach. Create targeted ad campaigns that drive traffic to your website or specific landing pages with affiliate links.

3. Email Marketing:
Email marketing allows you to nurture and build relationships with your audience, promote your affiliate products, and drive conversions. Consider the following email marketing strategies:

a) Building an Email List: Create lead magnets, such as free e-books or exclusive content, to encourage visitors to subscribe to your email list. Offer valuable content, product updates, and exclusive offers to your subscribers.

b) Segmentation: Segment your email list based on subscriber interests, preferences, or purchasing behavior. This allows you to tailor your email campaigns and promote relevant affiliate products to specific segments of your audience.

c) Email Automation: Set up automated email sequences or drip campaigns to deliver targeted and timely content to your subscribers. Use automation tools to schedule and personalize your email campaigns based on subscriber actions or triggers.

d) Promotional Emails: Periodically send dedicated promotional emails highlighting your affiliate products, exclusive discounts, or limited-time offers. Craft compelling subject lines and persuasive copy to entice subscribers to click and make purchases.

4. Search Engine Marketing (SEM):
Search engine marketing involves paid advertising to increase your website's visibility in search engine results. Consider the following SEM strategies:

a) Pay-Per-Click (PPC) Advertising: Utilize platforms like Google Ads or Bing Ads to create targeted ad campaigns. Select relevant keywords, create compelling ad copy, and drive traffic directly to your affiliate landing pages.

b) Display Advertising: Display ads on relevant websites or within ad networks to increase brand visibility and attract targeted visitors. Use visually appealing graphics and persuasive ad copy to grab attention and generate clicks.

c) Remarketing Campaigns: Implement remarketing campaigns to re-engage visitors who have previously shown interest in your website or products. Show targeted ads to these users across various platforms to remind them of the products they were interested in.

5. Influencer Marketing:
Leverage the influence of popular individuals or industry experts to promote your affiliate products. Consider the following influencer marketing strategies:

a) Affiliate Partnerships: Collaborate with influencers and offer them an affiliate partnership. Provide them with unique affiliate links or discount codes to promote to their audience. This allows you to tap into their trust and credibility.

b) Sponsored Content: Sponsor influencer-created content such as blog posts, videos, or social media posts that feature your affiliate products. Ensure the content aligns with your brand and resonates with the influencer's audience.

c) Giveaways and Contests: Organize giveaways or contests in collaboration with influencers. This can generate excitement, increase brand exposure, and attract new visitors to your website or social media channels.

Conclusion:
Implementing various marketing channels is crucial for affiliate marketers to effectively promote their affiliate products and maximize their success. By leveraging content marketing, social media marketing, email marketing, search engine marketing, and influencer marketing, you can reach a wider audience, engage with your target audience, and drive traffic to your affiliate links. Remember to consistently evaluate the performance of your marketing channels, analyze data, and refine your strategies based on user feedback and industry trends to optimize your affiliate marketing efforts.

- Harnessing the power of content marketing, social media, email marketing, and paid advertising.

Harnessing the power of content marketing, social media, email marketing, and paid advertising is key to maximizing your reach, engagement, and conversions in affiliate marketing. By utilizing these powerful marketing channels effectively, you can build brand awareness, engage your target audience, nurture relationships, and drive traffic to your affiliate products. In this chapter, we will explore strategies for harnessing the power of content marketing, social media, email marketing, and paid advertising to enhance your affiliate marketing efforts.

1. Content Marketing:
Content marketing involves creating and distributing valuable and relevant content to attract and engage your audience. Consider the following strategies:

a) Blogging: Maintain a blog where you consistently publish informative and engaging articles related to your niche and affiliate products. Incorporate targeted keywords and include affiliate links naturally within your content.

b) SEO Optimization: Optimize your blog posts and website content for search engines to improve visibility and organic traffic. Conduct keyword research, optimize meta tags, headings, and URLs, and focus on providing valuable information to your audience.

c) Guest Posting: Contribute guest posts to reputable websites or blogs within your niche. This allows you to tap into their established audience, build credibility, and drive referral traffic to your own website or landing pages.

d) Video Content: Create engaging video content on platforms like YouTube or social media channels. Produce product reviews, tutorials, or informative videos that showcase the benefits and usage of your affiliate products. Include affiliate links in video descriptions or annotations.

2. Social Media Marketing:
Social media platforms offer vast opportunities to connect with your audience, build brand awareness, and drive traffic to your affiliate products. Consider the following strategies:

a) Platform Selection: Identify the social media platforms that align with your target audience. Focus on building a strong presence and engaging with your audience on platforms such as Facebook, Instagram, Twitter, LinkedIn, or Pinterest.

b) Content Sharing: Regularly share valuable content, including blog posts, videos, product recommendations, or industry news, on your social media profiles. Use eye-catching visuals, compelling captions, and relevant hashtags to attract attention and drive engagement.

c) Community Engagement: Actively engage with your audience by responding to comments, messages, and mentions. Encourage conversations, ask for feedback, and provide valuable insights to foster a sense of community and build relationships.

d) Paid Social Media Advertising: Utilize paid social media advertising options to expand your reach and target specific demographics. Create targeted ad campaigns that drive traffic to your website or specific landing pages with affiliate links.

3. Email Marketing:
Email marketing allows you to nurture relationships, deliver personalized content, and promote your affiliate products directly to your subscribers. Consider the following strategies:

a) Building an Email List: Create lead magnets, such as e-books, checklists, or exclusive content, to encourage visitors to subscribe to your email list. Provide valuable content and offers to your subscribers to nurture the relationship.

b) Segmentation and Personalization: Segment your email list based on subscriber interests, preferences, or purchasing behavior. Customize your email campaigns to deliver relevant content and product recommendations to specific segments of your audience.

c) Automation and Drip Campaigns: Set up automated email sequences or drip campaigns to deliver targeted and timely content to your subscribers. Use automation tools to schedule and personalize your email campaigns based on subscriber actions or triggers.

d) Promotional Emails: Send dedicated promotional emails highlighting your affiliate products, exclusive discounts, or limited-time offers. Craft compelling subject lines and persuasive copy to entice subscribers to click and make purchases through your affiliate links.

4. Paid Advertising:
Paid advertising allows you to reach a wider audience and drive targeted traffic to your affiliate products. Consider the following paid advertising strategies:

a) Pay-Per-Click (PPC) Advertising: Utilize platforms like Google Ads or Bing Ads to create targeted ad campaigns. Select relevant keywords, create compelling ad copy, and drive traffic directly to your affiliate landing pages.

b) Display Advertising: Place display ads on relevant websites or within ad networks to increase brand visibility and attract targeted visitors. Use visually appealing graphics and persuasive ad copy to grab attention and generate clicks.

c) Remarketing Campaigns: Implement remarketing campaigns to re-engage users who have previously shown interest in your website or affiliate products. Show targeted ads to these users across various platforms, reminding them of the products they were interested in.

d) Influencer Collaborations: Collaborate with influencers or micro-influencers within your niche. Partner with them to promote your affiliate products through sponsored posts, reviews, or giveaways. Leverage their audience and credibility to increase brand exposure and drive conversions.

Conclusion:

Harnessing the power of content marketing, social media, email marketing, and paid advertising is essential for maximizing your affiliate marketing success. By creating valuable content, optimizing it for search engines, leveraging social media platforms, building relationships through email marketing, and utilizing paid advertising channels, you can expand your reach, engage your audience, and drive targeted traffic to your affiliate products. Remember to monitor and analyze the performance of your marketing efforts, optimize your strategies based on data insights and user feedback, and continuously refine your approaches to achieve the best results in your affiliate marketing journey.

- Leveraging SEO techniques to improve your website's visibility and ranking.

Leveraging SEO (Search Engine Optimization) techniques is crucial for improving your website's visibility and ranking in search engine results. By optimizing your website and its content, you can attract organic traffic, reach your target audience, and increase the chances of conversions in your affiliate marketing efforts. In this chapter, we will explore effective SEO techniques that can help you enhance your website's visibility and ranking.

1. Keyword Research:
Keyword research forms the foundation of your SEO strategy. Consider the following strategies:

a) Identify Targeted Keywords: Research and identify relevant keywords and phrases that align with your niche, target audience, and search intent. Use keyword research tools to discover popular and low-competition keywords.

b) Long-Tail Keywords: Focus on long-tail keywords, which are more specific and have lower competition. Long-tail keywords allow you to target a more targeted audience and increase the chances of ranking higher in search results.

c) Competitive Analysis: Analyze the keywords your competitors are targeting and consider incorporating them into your SEO strategy. Look for keyword gaps or untapped opportunities that can give you a competitive advantage.

d) User Intent: Understand the intent behind the keywords your target audience is using. Are they looking for information, ready to make a purchase, or seeking comparisons? Tailor your content to match their intent and provide the most relevant information.

2. On-Page Optimization:
On-page optimization involves optimizing various elements on your website to improve

search engine visibility. Consider the following strategies:

a) Title Tags and Meta Descriptions: Optimize your title tags and meta descriptions with targeted keywords, ensuring they accurately describe the content on each page. This helps search engines understand the relevance of your content to user queries.

b) Heading Tags: Use proper heading tags (H1, H2, H3, etc.) to structure your content. Incorporate targeted keywords in your headings to improve readability and signal the importance of your content to search engines.

c) URL Structure: Create SEO-friendly URLs that include relevant keywords and are descriptive of the page's content. Avoid using long and complex URLs with unnecessary parameters.

d) Internal Linking: Incorporate internal links within your content to guide users to related articles or product pages on your website. Internal linking improves website navigation, helps search engines discover content, and improves the overall user experience.

3. High-Quality Content:

Producing high-quality, valuable, and relevant content is essential for SEO success. Consider the following strategies:

a) Informative and Engaging Content: Create content that provides valuable information, answers user queries, and engages your audience. Aim to become an authority in your niche by delivering unique insights, tips, and solutions.

b) Keyword Optimization: Incorporate targeted keywords naturally into your content, including headings, subheadings, paragraphs, and image alt tags. Avoid keyword stuffing, as it can negatively impact user experience and search engine rankings.

c) Readability and Formatting: Use proper formatting techniques with clear headings, bullet points, and paragraphs to enhance readability. Break up your content into digestible sections, making it easier for users to scan and find relevant information.

d) Multimedia Integration: Enhance your content with high-quality images, videos, infographics, or interactive elements. Visual content can increase engagement, improve user experience, and make your content more shareable.

4. Website Performance and Technical Optimization:
Ensuring your website performs well and is technically optimized is crucial for SEO. Consider the following strategies:

a) Page Speed: Optimize your website's loading speed by compressing images, minifying code, leveraging browser caching, and utilizing content delivery networks (CDNs). Faster-loading websites have a better chance of ranking higher in search results.

b) Mobile-Friendliness: Ensure your website is responsive and mobile-friendly. With the increasing number of mobile users, having a mobile-friendly website is essential for both user experience and search engine rankings.

c) Website Architecture: Create a logical and organized website structure that is easy for search engines to crawl and index. Use XML sitemaps, clear navigation, and breadcrumbs to help search engines understand your website's structure.

d) Secure Website: Implement SSL certificates (HTTPS) to secure your website. Secure websites are preferred by search engines and provide a safer browsing experience for users.

5. Link Building:
Link building plays a vital role in SEO by increasing your website's authority and credibility. Consider the following strategies:

a) High-Quality Backlinks: Focus on acquiring high-quality backlinks from reputable and relevant websites within your niche. Seek opportunities for guest blogging, collaborations, or industry associations to build authoritative backlinks.

b) Content Promotion: Promote your high-quality content through outreach, social media, and influencer collaborations. Compelling content is more likely to attract natural backlinks from other websites.

c) Internal Linking: Strategically link to relevant internal pages within your content. Internal linking helps search engines understand the hierarchy and importance of your pages, improving overall website visibility.

d) Monitor and Disavow: Regularly monitor your backlink profile to identify low-quality or spammy links. Use the Google Disavow tool to disassociate your website from such links and maintain a healthy backlink profile.

Conclusion:

Leveraging SEO techniques is crucial for improving your website's visibility and ranking in search engine results. By conducting keyword research, optimizing on-page elements, producing high-quality content, ensuring technical optimization, and implementing effective link building strategies, you can enhance your website's visibility, attract organic traffic, and maximize your affiliate marketing success. Stay up-to-date with SEO best practices, monitor your website's performance, and adapt your strategies based on user feedback and search engine algorithm updates to maintain a competitive edge in the evolving digital landscape.

- Establishing Credibility and Trust:

Establishing credibility and trust is crucial for affiliate marketers to build a loyal audience, attract customers, and succeed in their niche. By focusing on building your personal brand and positioning yourself as an authority, you can gain the trust of your target audience and differentiate yourself from competitors. In this chapter, we will explore strategies for establishing credibility, building your personal brand, and positioning yourself as an authority in your niche.

1. Define Your Niche and Expertise:
To establish credibility, it is important to define your niche and expertise. Consider the following strategies:

a) Identify Your Niche: Determine the specific area within your industry that you want to focus on. Find a niche that aligns with your interests, expertise, and target audience's needs.

b) Research and Stay Informed: Continuously educate yourself about your niche through research, industry news, and staying up-to-date with the latest trends. Become an expert in your field and stay ahead of industry developments.

c) Specialize and Differentiate: Identify your unique selling points and find ways to differentiate yourself from competitors. Focus on a specific aspect of your niche where you can provide exceptional value or expertise.

2. Build Your Personal Brand:
Building a strong personal brand helps establish credibility and makes you memorable to your audience. Consider the following strategies:

a) Define Your Brand Identity: Determine your brand values, mission statement, and unique voice. Develop a consistent brand identity that aligns with your niche and resonates with your target audience.

b) Consistent Branding: Implement your brand identity across all your online platforms, including your website, social media profiles, email newsletters, and content. Use consistent visuals, messaging, and tone of voice to create a cohesive brand experience.

c) Authenticity and Transparency: Be authentic and transparent in your interactions with your audience. Show your personality, share personal stories, and be genuine in your communication. Building trust requires authenticity.

d) Engage with Your Audience: Actively engage with your audience through social media, comments, and email. Respond to their questions, comments, and concerns, and show that you genuinely care about their needs and experiences.

3. Content Creation and Thought Leadership: Establishing yourself as an authority requires creating valuable content and demonstrating thought leadership. Consider the following strategies:

a) Create High-Quality Content: Produce high-quality, informative, and engaging content that provides value to your audience. Share your expertise, insights, and unique perspectives through blog posts, videos, podcasts, or other mediums.

b) Consistency and Regularity: Maintain a consistent content creation schedule to build momentum and keep your audience engaged. Regularly publish content that addresses their pain points, answers their questions, and provides solutions.

c) Thought Leadership: Share your expertise and unique insights through thought leadership content. Provide innovative ideas, strategies, or perspectives that differentiate you from others in your niche. Show your audience that you are at the forefront of industry knowledge.

d) Guest Contributions: Contribute guest posts or participate in industry podcasts or webinars to showcase your expertise. Collaborate with other influencers or thought leaders in your niche to expand your reach and credibility.

4. Social Proof and Testimonials:

Social proof plays a vital role in establishing credibility and trust. Consider the following strategies:

a) Customer Testimonials: Collect and showcase testimonials from satisfied customers or clients. Highlight their positive experiences, results, and feedback. Testimonials act as social proof and build trust with your audience.

b) Case Studies and Success Stories: Share real-life case studies or success stories that demonstrate the effectiveness of the products or services you promote. Provide detailed examples of how your recommendations have helped people achieve their goals.

c) Influencer Collaborations: Collaborate with influencers or industry experts within your niche. Partnering with respected individuals can enhance your credibility and introduce you to a wider audience.

d) Affiliate Product Reviews: Create comprehensive and unbiased reviews of the affiliate products you promote. Offer honest assessments, share personal experiences, and provide valuable insights. Transparency in your reviews builds trust with your audience.

Conclusion:
Establishing credibility and trust is essential for affiliate marketers to build a loyal audience and succeed in their niche. By defining your niche, building a strong personal brand, creating valuable content, and showcasing social proof, you can position yourself as an authority and gain the trust of your target audience. Remember to consistently deliver high-quality content, engage with your audience, and provide transparent and authentic interactions. Building credibility takes time and effort, but it is a valuable investment that will contribute to your long-term success as an affiliate marketer.

- Creating valuable and informative content that positions you as a trusted expert.

Creating valuable and informative content is a powerful strategy for establishing yourself as a trusted expert in your niche. By consistently delivering high-quality content that addresses your audience's needs, provides valuable insights, and positions you as a go-to resource, you can build trust, credibility, and a loyal following. In this chapter, we will explore strategies for creating content that positions you as a trusted expert in your field.

1. Understand Your Audience:
To create valuable content, it is essential to have a deep understanding of your target audience. Consider the following strategies:

a) Research: Conduct thorough research to identify your audience's needs, pain points, and interests. Understand their challenges, goals, and the information they seek within your niche.

b) Audience Personas: Develop detailed audience personas to represent different segments of your target audience. This helps you tailor your content to their specific needs and preferences.

c) Feedback and Engagement: Engage with your audience through comments, social media interactions, and surveys to gather feedback and gain insights into their preferences, questions, and concerns.

d) Keyword Analysis: Conduct keyword research to identify the topics and keywords that your audience is searching for. This helps you create content that is relevant and aligns with their search intent.

2. Provide Valuable Insights and Expertise: Creating content that provides valuable insights and demonstrates your expertise is key to positioning yourself as a trusted expert. Consider the following strategies:

a) In-Depth Guides and Tutorials: Create comprehensive guides and tutorials that delve deep into specific topics within your niche.

Offer step-by-step instructions, practical tips, and actionable advice.

b) Thought Leadership Content: Share your unique perspectives, industry insights, and innovative ideas through thought leadership content. Provide in-depth analysis, thought-provoking ideas, and predictions within your niche.

c) Case Studies and Success Stories: Share real-life case studies and success stories that highlight how your expertise and recommendations have helped others achieve their goals. Provide data, examples, and testimonials to demonstrate the effectiveness of your strategies.

d) Original Research and Data: Conduct original research within your niche and present the findings through data-driven content. This positions you as a trusted source of accurate and valuable information.

3. Engage and Educate Your Audience:

Engaging and educating your audience is crucial for establishing trust and credibility. Consider the following strategies:

a) Interactive Content: Create interactive content such as quizzes, assessments, or surveys that allow your audience to actively participate and gain insights. This fosters engagement and interaction with your brand.

b) Q&A Sessions and Live Streams: Host live Q&A sessions or live streams where you can directly interact with your audience, answer their questions, and provide valuable insights. This builds rapport and positions you as a knowledgeable expert.

c) Webinars and Online Workshops: Organize webinars or online workshops to share your expertise, provide in-depth training, and offer practical advice. These interactive sessions allow you to engage with your audience in real-time and establish yourself as a trusted educator.

d) Community Building: Create an online community, such as a forum, Facebook group, or Slack channel, where your audience can connect, ask questions, and share insights. Actively participate in discussions and provide valuable input to foster a sense of community and build trust.

4. Consistency and Quality:
Consistency and maintaining high-quality standards are key to establishing yourself as a trusted expert. Consider the following strategies:

a) Content Calendar: Develop a content calendar to plan and organize your content creation. Consistency in publishing helps you build credibility and keeps your audience engaged.

b) Well-Researched Content: Conduct thorough research, gather data, and use reputable sources to ensure the accuracy and reliability of your content. Fact-check your information to maintain your credibility.

c) Engaging Writing Style: Develop a writing style that is clear, engaging, and easy to understand. Use storytelling techniques, examples, and analogies to make complex concepts more accessible to your audience.

d) Multimedia Integration: Enhance your content with multimedia elements such as images, infographics, videos, or podcasts. This diversifies your content and caters to different learning preferences.

Conclusion:
Creating valuable and informative content is instrumental in establishing yourself as a trusted expert in your niche. By understanding your audience, providing valuable insights and expertise, engaging and educating your audience, and maintaining consistency and quality in your content, you can position yourself as a go-to resource for your target audience. Remember to continuously research, engage with your audience, and stay up-to-date with industry trends to ensure your content remains valuable and relevant. Building trust takes time and effort, but the rewards are a loyal audience, increased credibility, and long-term success in your field as a trusted expert.

- Utilizing testimonials and reviews to enhance credibility and gain trust from your audience.

Utilizing testimonials and reviews is a powerful strategy for enhancing credibility and gaining trust from your audience in affiliate marketing. Positive feedback and experiences from satisfied customers or clients serve as social proof, demonstrating the value and reliability of the products or services you promote. In this chapter, we will explore effective ways to utilize testimonials and reviews to enhance your credibility and build trust with your audience.

1. Collecting Authentic Testimonials: Authentic testimonials from satisfied customers or clients can significantly boost your credibility. Consider the following strategies:

a) Request Feedback: Reach out to customers or clients and request feedback on their experience with the products or services you recommended. Ask specific questions that allow them to highlight the benefits and results they achieved.

b) Follow-Up Emails: Send follow-up emails to customers after they have made a purchase, seeking their feedback and encouraging them to share their experience. Make the process as easy and convenient as possible by providing clear instructions or a feedback form.

c) Social Media Reviews: Encourage customers to leave reviews or testimonials on your social media platforms. Create posts asking for feedback and provide a link or instructions on how to leave a review. Monitor and respond to reviews to show that you value customer feedback.

d) Affiliate Program Reviews: Encourage your affiliate partners to leave reviews or testimonials about their experience working with you. Their positive feedback can reflect your professionalism, reliability, and the value you bring to their business.

2. Displaying Testimonials Strategically:

Displaying testimonials in a strategic manner can maximize their impact on your audience's trust. Consider the following strategies:

a) Dedicated Testimonials Page: Create a dedicated page on your website to showcase testimonials from satisfied customers or clients. Arrange the testimonials in a visually appealing format, including the customer's name, photo (if available), and a brief description of their experience.

b) Incorporating Testimonials in Content: Integrate testimonials within your blog posts, product reviews, or landing pages. Place them strategically to highlight the benefits, results, or positive experiences associated with the products or services you promote.

c) Video Testimonials: Encourage customers to provide video testimonials sharing their positive experiences and results. Embed these video testimonials on your website or share them on social media platforms to increase credibility and engagement.

d) Case Studies: Use case studies that showcase in-depth success stories, including testimonials, data, and before-and-after results. These detailed accounts demonstrate how your recommended products or services have positively impacted real people.

3. Highlighting Authenticity and Relevance: Emphasizing the authenticity and relevance of testimonials and reviews helps build trust with your audience. Consider the following strategies:

a) Use Real Names and Photos: Whenever possible, include the customer's real name and photo in the testimonials. This adds authenticity and helps your audience connect with real people who have had positive experiences.

b) Include Specific Details: Encourage customers to provide specific details about their experience, such as the problem they faced, how the product or service helped them, and the results they achieved. Specificity adds credibility and relatability.

c) Segment Testimonials: Categorize testimonials based on the specific products or services you promote. This allows your audience to find testimonials that are relevant to their needs, making them more likely to trust the recommendations.

d) Share Diverse Testimonials: Aim to include testimonials from various demographics, industries, or customer segments. Showcasing a diverse range of positive experiences demonstrates the broad appeal and effectiveness of the products or services you recommend.

4. Responding to Feedback:
Responding to testimonials and reviews demonstrates your commitment to customer satisfaction and further enhances your credibility. Consider the following strategies:

a) Thank and Acknowledge: Respond to each testimonial or review with gratitude and appreciation. Thank the customer for their feedback and express your happiness in hearing about their positive experience.

b) Address Concerns: If you receive any negative feedback or constructive criticism, respond promptly and professionally. Show empathy, acknowledge their concerns, and offer solutions or assistance to resolve the issue.

c) Encourage Dialogue: Encourage customers to engage in a conversation by responding to their testimonials or reviews. Ask follow-up questions, request additional details, or invite them to share their experience further.

d) Share Testimonials on Social Media: Highlight testimonials on your social media platforms by sharing them as posts or creating graphics. Tag and mention the customers who provided the testimonials, further showcasing their positive experiences.

Conclusion:

Utilizing testimonials and reviews effectively can enhance your credibility and build trust with your audience in affiliate marketing. By collecting authentic testimonials, strategically displaying them, highlighting authenticity and relevance, and responding to feedback, you demonstrate the value and reliability of the products or services you recommend. Testimonials serve as powerful social proof and play a crucial role in influencing purchasing decisions. Embrace the positive feedback from your satisfied customers or clients to strengthen your reputation, build trust, and attract new customers to your affiliate products.

- Maximizing Conversions and Sales:

Maximizing conversions and sales is the ultimate goal of affiliate marketing. By implementing effective strategies and optimizing your approach, you can increase the likelihood of turning your website visitors into customers and generating revenue through affiliate commissions. In this chapter, we will explore strategies for maximizing conversions and sales in affiliate marketing.

1. Understand Your Target Audience: Understanding your target audience is crucial for optimizing conversions. Consider the following strategies:

a) Market Research: Conduct thorough market research to identify your audience's needs, preferences, and pain points. Understand their motivations, demographics, and purchasing behavior.

b) Buyer Personas: Develop detailed buyer personas that represent different segments of your target audience. Tailor your content, promotions, and recommendations to align with each persona's preferences and goals.

c) User Insights: Utilize analytics tools to gather insights on user behavior, such as click-through rates, time spent on page, and conversion rates. Analyze this data to understand how users are interacting with your content and identify areas for improvement.

d) Surveys and Feedback: Engage with your audience through surveys, feedback forms, or social media interactions to gather valuable insights. Ask for feedback on their purchase decisions, pain points, and suggestions for improvement.

2. Strategic Product Selection:
Choosing the right affiliate products to promote is essential for maximizing conversions. Consider the following strategies:

a) Relevance and Alignment: Select products that are relevant to your niche and align with your audience's interests and needs. The more closely the products match their desires, the higher the chances of conversion.

b) Quality and Reputation: Promote products from reputable merchants with a proven track record of quality and customer satisfaction. Positive reviews, testimonials, and ratings can help build trust and increase conversions.

c) Product Research: Conduct thorough research on the products you plan to promote. Understand their features, benefits, and potential drawbacks. Consider testing the products yourself to provide firsthand experiences and recommendations.

d) Diversify Product Portfolio: Offer a range of products within your niche to cater to different preferences and needs. This diversification can help capture a larger audience and increase the likelihood of conversions.

3. Compelling Content and Call-to-Actions: Creating compelling content and using effective call-to-actions (CTAs) can significantly impact conversions. Consider the following strategies:

a) High-Quality Content: Produce informative, engaging, and persuasive content that addresses your audience's pain points and showcases the benefits of the affiliate products. Use storytelling techniques, visuals, and examples to captivate your audience.

b) Product Reviews and Comparisons: Create detailed and unbiased product reviews that provide an objective evaluation of the pros and cons. Include comparisons with similar products to help users make informed decisions.

c) Persuasive CTAs: Use persuasive and action-oriented language in your CTAs to encourage users to take the desired action. Make them stand out visually, and place them strategically within your content or on prominent areas of your website.

d) Urgency and Scarcity: Create a sense of urgency or scarcity by highlighting limited-time offers, exclusive discounts, or product availability. This can motivate users to take immediate action and increase conversions.

4. Optimization and Testing:
Continuously optimizing and testing your strategies is vital for maximizing conversions. Consider the following strategies:

a) A/B Testing: Conduct A/B tests to compare different variations of your content, CTAs, landing pages, or promotional strategies. Analyze the results to identify the most effective elements that drive conversions.

b) Conversion Tracking: Utilize conversion tracking tools to monitor and measure the effectiveness of your affiliate campaigns. Track key metrics such as click-through rates, conversion rates, and revenue generated.

c) Landing Page Optimization: Optimize your landing pages by removing distractions, improving load times, and enhancing the overall user experience. A clear and compelling landing page can significantly increase conversions.

d) Continuous Improvement: Regularly analyze your data, user feedback, and industry trends to identify areas for improvement.

Experiment with new strategies, content formats, or promotional techniques to refine your approach and maximize conversions.

5. Building Trust and Relationships:
Building trust and fostering relationships with your audience is essential for driving conversions. Consider the following strategies:

a) Transparency and Honesty: Be transparent about your affiliate partnerships and disclose any potential biases or conflicts of interest. Honesty builds trust and establishes you as a credible source of information.

b) Authentic Communication: Communicate authentically with your audience, addressing their concerns, and providing reliable and unbiased recommendations. Engage in conversations, respond to comments, and build a sense of community.

c) Social Proof: Highlight testimonials, reviews, and success stories from satisfied customers to provide social proof. Showcase the positive experiences others have had with the affiliate products you promote.

d) Customer Support and Follow-Up: Provide excellent customer support and follow-up with customers who have made purchases through your affiliate links. Offer assistance, answer their questions, and provide value even after the initial transaction.

Conclusion:
Maximizing conversions and sales is a critical aspect of affiliate marketing success. By understanding your target audience, strategically selecting products, creating compelling content, optimizing your strategies, and building trust and relationships, you can increase your chances of converting website visitors into customers. Remember to continuously analyze data, test different approaches, and adapt your strategies based on user feedback and industry trends. With a customer-centric approach and a commitment to delivering value, you can optimize conversions and drive revenue through your affiliate marketing efforts.

- Understanding the customer journey and implementing effective sales funnels.

Understanding the customer journey and implementing effective sales funnels are crucial steps in maximizing conversions and sales in affiliate marketing. By mapping out the path that customers take from initial awareness to making a purchase, you can strategically guide them through the sales process and optimize your marketing efforts. In this chapter, we will explore the customer journey and discuss how to implement effective sales funnels in your affiliate marketing strategy.

1. Customer Journey Stages:
The customer journey consists of several stages, and understanding each stage helps you tailor your marketing strategies accordingly. Consider the following stages:

a) Awareness: At this stage, potential customers become aware of their needs or a problem they want to solve. They may discover your brand or products through search engines, social media, referrals, or content marketing efforts.

b) Consideration: In the consideration stage, customers actively research and compare different solutions or products to address their needs. They evaluate options, read reviews, seek recommendations, and explore different sources of information.

c) Decision: The decision stage is when customers are ready to make a purchase. They have narrowed down their options and are looking for the best deal, reliable recommendations, or additional incentives that can influence their final decision.

d) Post-Purchase: After making a purchase, customers enter the post-purchase stage. This is an opportunity to provide exceptional customer service, follow-up support, and encourage loyalty or repeat purchases.

2. Implementing Sales Funnels:
Sales funnels help guide potential customers through each stage of the customer journey, optimizing the conversion process. Consider the following strategies:

a) Create Engaging and Relevant Content: At the awareness stage, focus on creating informative and engaging content that attracts your target audience. This can include blog posts, videos, social media content, or lead magnets that provide value and address their pain points.

b) Capture Leads and Nurture Relationships: Offer lead magnets such as e-books, checklists, or exclusive content to capture leads in the consideration stage. Use email marketing to nurture relationships, provide additional information, and showcase the benefits of the affiliate products you promote.

c) Landing Pages and Opt-In Forms: Create dedicated landing pages with compelling copy and visually appealing designs. Include opt-in forms to collect contact information and offer incentives to encourage sign-ups, such as exclusive discounts or free trials.

d) Personalized Email Campaigns: Segment your email list based on the customer's stage in the journey and deliver personalized content. Provide relevant information, product recommendations, testimonials, or limited-time offers to move them closer to making a purchase.

e) Product Reviews and Comparisons: At the consideration stage, offer detailed product reviews and comparisons to help customers evaluate their options. Highlight the unique features, benefits, and value propositions of the affiliate products you promote.

f) Call-to-Action (CTA) Optimization: Place strategic CTAs throughout your content, landing pages, and emails to guide customers towards the decision stage. Use persuasive language, urgency, and clear instructions to encourage them to take the desired action.

g) Seamless Checkout and Purchase Process: Ensure a smooth and user-friendly checkout process when customers are ready to make a purchase. Optimize your affiliate links, ensure website security, and provide multiple payment options for convenience.

h) Post-Purchase Follow-Up: After customers make a purchase, continue to engage with them. Send follow-up emails with order confirmations, delivery updates, and post-purchase support. Offer additional resources, exclusive content, or loyalty programs to encourage repeat purchases.

3. Analyze and Optimize:
Regularly analyze data and metrics to identify areas for improvement and optimize your sales funnels. Consider the following strategies:

a) Conversion Tracking: Utilize conversion tracking tools to measure key metrics such as click-through rates, conversion rates, and revenue generated. Identify the stages or specific steps where customers drop off and make adjustments accordingly.

b) A/B Testing: Conduct A/B tests to compare different variations of your landing pages, CTAs, email subject lines, or content formats. Analyze the results to identify the most effective elements that drive conversions and refine your strategies accordingly.

c) Customer Feedback: Collect feedback from customers to understand their experience throughout the customer journey. Use surveys, polls, or social media interactions to gather insights on pain points, preferences, and suggestions for improvement.

d) Continuous Optimization: Continuously optimize your sales funnels based on the data and feedback you collect. Test new strategies, experiment with different approaches, and refine your content, CTAs, or email sequences to improve the overall conversion rates and sales.

Conclusion:
Understanding the customer journey and implementing effective sales funnels are essential for maximizing conversions and sales in affiliate marketing. By mapping out the stages of the customer journey, implementing strategies tailored to each stage, and continuously analyzing and optimizing your efforts, you can guide potential customers through the conversion process more effectively. Remember to create engaging and relevant content, capture leads, nurture relationships, provide valuable information, and offer a seamless purchasing experience. By

aligning your marketing efforts with the customer journey, you can increase conversions, build customer loyalty, and drive revenue through your affiliate marketing endeavors.

- Utilizing persuasive copywriting techniques to drive conversions.

Persuasive copywriting is a powerful tool in affiliate marketing that can significantly impact conversions. By employing persuasive techniques, you can engage your audience, communicate the value of the products or services you promote, and compel them to take action. In this chapter, we will explore effective persuasive copywriting techniques that can help you drive conversions in your affiliate marketing efforts.

1. Understand Your Audience:
Understanding your audience is the foundation of persuasive copywriting. Consider the following strategies:

a) Buyer Personas: Develop detailed buyer personas that represent different segments of your target audience. Understand their motivations, pain points, desires, and values.

b) Language and Tone: Use language and a tone of voice that resonates with your audience. Speak their language, mirror their style of communication, and use words that evoke emotions or convey value.

c) Research and Feedback: Conduct research, gather data, and seek feedback from your audience. Understand their needs, preferences, and the language they use to describe their challenges and desires.

d) Empathy and Empathetic Writing: Put yourself in your audience's shoes and demonstrate empathy in your writing. Show that you understand their struggles and present your solutions as the answer to their problems.

2. Compelling Headlines and Openers: Capturing your audience's attention from the beginning is crucial in persuasive copywriting. Consider the following strategies:

a) Intriguing Headlines: Craft attention-grabbing headlines that create curiosity, offer a benefit, or pose a compelling question. Make it clear how your content or the product you're promoting can address your audience's needs.

b) Storytelling Openers: Begin your copy with a captivating story or anecdote that relates to your audience's pain points or desires. Engage their emotions and make them invested in what you have to say.

c) Problem Identification: Highlight the problem your audience is facing and emphasize the pain or challenges associated with it. This creates a sense of urgency and positions your solution as the remedy.

d) Start with a Benefit: Communicate a clear benefit or solution right from the start. Show your audience the value they will gain by engaging with your content or taking action.

3. Features vs. Benefits:
Emphasizing the benefits of the products or services you promote is key to persuasive copywriting. Consider the following strategies:

a) Benefits-Driven Language: Focus on the benefits your audience will experience rather than just listing the features. Clearly communicate how the product or service solves their problems or fulfills their desires.

b) Use of Emotional Triggers: Appeal to your audience's emotions by highlighting how the product or service will make them feel. Connect the benefits with their aspirations, happiness, security, or success.

c) Demonstration of Value: Quantify the value your audience will receive by using specific examples, statistics, or testimonials. Show them the tangible outcomes they can expect.

d) Paint a Picture: Use vivid language and descriptive storytelling to help your audience visualize the benefits they will experience. Make them imagine a future state where their problems are solved or desires are fulfilled.

4. Social Proof and Testimonials: Incorporating social proof and testimonials adds credibility and trust to your persuasive copy. Consider the following strategies:

a) Testimonials: Include authentic and compelling testimonials from satisfied customers or clients. Highlight their positive experiences, results, and the transformation they achieved through the product or service.

b) Case Studies: Present case studies that showcase real-life examples of success using the product or service. Describe the challenges, the journey, and the measurable outcomes achieved.

c) Influencer Endorsements: Utilize endorsements from respected influencers or industry experts. Their authority and credibility can reinforce your persuasive message and build trust with your audience.

d) User-Generated Content: Share user-generated content, such as reviews, ratings, or social media posts, that demonstrate positive experiences and engagement with the product or service. This provides social proof and builds trust.

5. Call-to-Action (CTA) Optimization:
A strong and persuasive call-to-action is essential for driving conversions. Consider the following strategies:

a) Clear and Actionable Language: Use clear and concise language that directs your audience to take the desired action. Avoid ambiguity and communicate the benefits of taking action.

b) Urgency and Scarcity: Create a sense of urgency or scarcity by emphasizing limited-time offers, exclusive deals, or limited availability. Encourage immediate action by showcasing the benefits of acting now.

c) Benefit-Driven CTAs: Align your call-to-action with the benefits your audience will gain by taking action. Highlight how the product or service will solve their problems or fulfill their desires.

d) Visual and Placement: Make your call-to-action stand out visually using contrasting colors, buttons, or graphics. Place it strategically in prominent areas of your copy or website where it is easily visible and accessible.

Conclusion:

Utilizing persuasive copywriting techniques is instrumental in driving conversions in affiliate marketing. By understanding your audience, crafting compelling headlines and openers, emphasizing benefits, incorporating social proof and testimonials, and optimizing your call-to-action, you can effectively engage your audience and compel them to take action. Remember to continuously refine your copywriting based on feedback, data, and testing. With persuasive copy, you can captivate your audience, communicate the value of the products or services you promote, and drive conversions in your affiliate marketing endeavors.

- Implementing call-to-actions, landing pages, and lead magnets to capture leads and increase sales.

Implementing effective call-to-actions (CTAs), landing pages, and lead magnets is essential for capturing leads and increasing sales in affiliate marketing. These elements play a crucial role in guiding your audience through the conversion process and encouraging them to take action. In this chapter, we will explore strategies for implementing CTAs, creating impactful landing pages, and offering compelling lead magnets to capture leads and boost sales in your affiliate marketing efforts.

1. Call-to-Actions (CTAs):
Call-to-actions are key prompts that encourage your audience to take a specific action. Consider the following strategies:

a) Clear and Compelling Language: Use clear and concise language that clearly communicates the desired action. Make your CTAs compelling by emphasizing the value or benefit your audience will receive by taking action.

b) Placement and Visibility: Position your CTAs strategically on your website, blog posts, emails, and social media profiles. Place them where they are highly visible, such as above the fold, at the end of a blog post, or within eye-catching buttons.

c) Visual Appeal: Make your CTAs visually appealing by using contrasting colors, eye-catching buttons, or engaging graphics. Ensure they stand out from the surrounding content and are easily recognizable.

d) Urgency and Scarcity: Create a sense of urgency or scarcity in your CTAs to motivate immediate action. Use phrases like "Limited Time Offer" or "Exclusive Deal" to instill a fear of missing out and encourage prompt engagement.

2. Landing Pages:
Landing pages are dedicated web pages designed to convert visitors into leads or customers. Consider the following strategies:

a) Clear Value Proposition: Clearly communicate the unique value proposition of your offer on the landing page. Explain how your product or service solves a specific problem or fulfills a need for your audience.

b) Minimal Distractions: Remove unnecessary distractions such as navigation menus, sidebars, or excessive links that might divert your visitors' attention away from the main offer. Keep the focus solely on the desired conversion goal.

c) Concise and Persuasive Copy: Craft concise and persuasive copy that highlights the benefits of your offer. Use compelling headlines, bullet points, and visuals to communicate the value and entice visitors to take action.

d) Trust Signals: Include trust signals such as customer testimonials, ratings, reviews, security badges, or certifications to build trust and credibility with your audience. These elements instill confidence in your offer.

3. Lead Magnets:

Lead magnets are valuable incentives that entice visitors to provide their contact information, enabling you to capture leads. Consider the following strategies:

a) Relevant and Valuable Content: Offer lead magnets that are directly related to your niche and provide high value to your audience. This can include e-books, whitepapers, checklists, templates, webinars, or exclusive content.

b) Compelling Opt-in Forms: Design visually appealing opt-in forms that clearly state the benefits of your lead magnet. Keep the form fields minimal, asking for only essential information to reduce friction and increase conversions.

c) Opt-in Placement: Place your opt-in forms strategically on your website, blog posts, or landing pages. Experiment with different placements to find the most effective positions for capturing leads.

d) Targeted Segmentation: Segment your lead magnets to align with specific buyer personas or audience segments. This allows you to offer personalized content and increase relevance, leading to higher opt-in rates.

4. Conversion Tracking and Optimization: Tracking and optimizing your CTAs, landing pages, and lead magnets is crucial for continuous improvement. Consider the following strategies:

a) Conversion Tracking: Utilize analytics tools and conversion tracking software to monitor the performance of your CTAs, landing pages, and lead magnets. Track metrics such as click-through rates, conversion rates, and lead generation.

b) A/B Testing: Conduct A/B tests to compare different variations of your CTAs, landing pages, or lead magnet offers. Test different headlines, copy, visuals, colors, or form layouts to identify the most effective elements for boosting conversions.

c) Data Analysis: Analyze the data gathered from your conversion tracking and A/B testing to gain insights into user behavior and preferences. Identify areas for improvement and make data-driven decisions to optimize your conversion strategies.

d) Continuous Optimization: Continuously refine your CTAs, landing pages, and lead magnets based on the insights and feedback you gather. Implement improvements, test new approaches, and iterate based on user response to maximize lead capture and sales.

Conclusion:
Implementing effective call-to-actions, landing pages, and lead magnets is essential for capturing leads and increasing sales in affiliate marketing. By creating compelling CTAs, designing impactful landing pages, and offering valuable lead magnets, you can engage your audience, guide them through the conversion process, and boost your affiliate sales. Remember to continuously track, analyze, and optimize your conversion strategies based on data and user feedback. With well-crafted CTAs, persuasive landing pages, and enticing lead magnets, you can effectively capture leads and increase your sales in the dynamic world of affiliate marketing.

Tracking and Analyzing Performance:

Tracking and analyzing affiliate marketing performance is crucial for optimizing your strategies, identifying areas of improvement, and achieving optimal results. By monitoring key metrics, analyzing data, and gaining insights into the effectiveness of your campaigns, you can make informed decisions and refine your approach. In this chapter, we will explore strategies for tracking and analyzing your affiliate marketing efforts to drive success.

1. Identify Key Performance Indicators (KPIs): Start by identifying the key metrics and performance indicators that align with your goals and objectives. Consider the following KPIs:

a) Click-through Rate (CTR): Measure the percentage of users who click on your affiliate links or ads. It indicates the effectiveness of your call-to-actions and the appeal of your marketing messages.

b) Conversion Rate: Calculate the percentage of visitors who complete a desired action, such as making a purchase or filling out a form. This metric reflects the effectiveness of your landing pages and product recommendations.

c) Revenue and Earnings: Monitor the revenue generated from your affiliate sales and track your earnings from commissions. This provides a clear picture of the financial impact of your marketing efforts.

d) Return on Investment (ROI): Assess the return on your investment by comparing the revenue generated with the resources and time invested. This helps evaluate the profitability of your affiliate marketing campaigns.

2. Utilize Tracking Tools and Platforms: Implement tracking tools and platforms to monitor your affiliate marketing performance accurately. Consider the following strategies:

a) Affiliate Network Tracking: Many affiliate networks provide tracking tools that offer detailed insights into clicks, conversions, and revenue. Utilize these tracking features to monitor the performance of your affiliate links.

b) Google Analytics: Integrate Google Analytics with your website to track user behavior, traffic sources, and conversions. Set up goals and funnels to monitor specific actions, such as completed purchases or lead generation.

c) URL Parameters and UTM Tags: Use unique URL parameters and UTM tags to track the performance of different marketing channels, campaigns, or promotional strategies. This enables you to identify the sources of traffic and conversions accurately.

d) Customized Dashboards: Create customized dashboards using analytics platforms like Google Data Studio or Microsoft Power BI. Consolidate key metrics and data visualizations in one place for easy monitoring and analysis.

3. Analyze Affiliate Reports and Data: Regularly analyze affiliate reports and data to gain insights into your performance and

identify areas for improvement. Consider the following strategies:

a) Conversion Funnel Analysis: Examine the steps users take from initial contact to conversion. Identify potential bottlenecks or drop-off points in the funnel and optimize those areas to maximize conversions.

b) Campaign and Channel Performance: Evaluate the performance of your campaigns and marketing channels. Identify the most effective channels in terms of conversions, revenue, and ROI. Allocate resources accordingly to optimize your efforts.

c) Product and Merchant Analysis: Analyze the performance of different products and merchants you promote. Identify the high-converting products, top-performing merchants, and opportunities for upselling or cross-selling.

d) Customer Segmentation: Segment your audience based on demographics, behavior, or preferences. Analyze the performance of each segment to understand their specific needs, purchasing patterns, and preferences.

4. Testing and Experimentation:
Conduct testing and experimentation to optimize your affiliate marketing strategies. Consider the following strategies:

a) A/B Testing: Test different variations of your landing pages, CTAs, email subject lines, or ad creatives to identify the most effective elements. Compare the performance of each variant and make data-driven decisions for optimization.

b) Affiliate Network and Program Testing: Explore different affiliate networks and programs to find the ones that align with your niche and offer higher commissions, better product selection, or advanced tracking features.

c) Promotional Strategies Testing: Experiment with different promotional strategies, such as content types, social media platforms, or email marketing approaches. Analyze the results to identify the strategies that generate the most engagement and conversions.

d) Continuous Improvement: Continuously refine your strategies based on data analysis and experimentation. Implement insights gained from testing and make iterative improvements to enhance your affiliate marketing performance.

5. Competitive Analysis:
Monitor and analyze the activities of your competitors to stay ahead in the affiliate marketing landscape. Consider the following strategies:

a) Competitor Research: Study the strategies, content, and promotions of your competitors in the same niche. Identify their strengths, weaknesses, and areas where you can differentiate yourself.

b) Affiliate Programs and Networks: Analyze the affiliate programs and networks your competitors are part of to identify lucrative opportunities or emerging trends.

c) Content Analysis: Evaluate the types of content your competitors produce, their engagement levels, and the affiliate products they promote. Identify gaps or areas where you can provide more value to your audience.

d) Offer Uniqueness: Differentiate yourself by offering unique value propositions, exclusive deals, or additional resources that set you apart from your competitors.

Conclusion:
Tracking and analyzing your affiliate marketing performance is a vital step in achieving optimal results. By identifying key performance indicators, utilizing tracking tools, analyzing reports and data, conducting testing and experimentation, and monitoring your competitors, you can gain valuable insights and make data-driven decisions to enhance your strategies. Regularly evaluate your performance, make iterative improvements, and adapt your approach based on the insights gained. With a proactive approach to tracking and analyzing, you can optimize your affiliate marketing efforts and drive success in this dynamic industry.

- Utilizing analytics tools to track and measure your affiliate marketing efforts.

Analytics tools are essential for tracking and measuring your affiliate marketing efforts. They provide valuable insights into the performance of your campaigns, help you understand user behavior, and enable data-driven decision-making. In this chapter, we will explore various analytics tools that can be utilized to track and measure your affiliate marketing efforts effectively.

1. Google Analytics:
Google Analytics is a widely used and robust web analytics platform that offers comprehensive insights into website performance and user behavior. Consider the following features and strategies:

a) Goal Tracking: Set up goals in Google Analytics to track specific actions, such as completed purchases, form submissions, or newsletter sign-ups. This allows you to measure the effectiveness of your affiliate marketing efforts.

b) E-commerce Tracking: Utilize e-commerce tracking to measure revenue, transactions, and conversion rates associated with your affiliate sales. Link your affiliate links or product pages with e-commerce tracking to gain insights into revenue generation.

c) Traffic Sources: Analyze the sources of your website traffic to understand which channels or campaigns are driving the most visitors. Identify the channels that generate the highest conversions and focus your efforts accordingly.

d) Behavior Flow: Use the Behavior Flow report to visualize how visitors navigate through your website. Identify popular entry and exit points, as well as the paths users take to complete desired actions or conversions.

2. Affiliate Network and Platform Analytics: Many affiliate networks and platforms provide their own analytics tools to track and measure your affiliate marketing performance. Consider the following features and strategies:

a) Click-through Rates (CTR): Monitor the CTR of your affiliate links or banners to understand the effectiveness of your promotional efforts. Identify the campaigns or placements that generate the highest CTRs and optimize accordingly.

b) Conversion Tracking: Utilize the conversion tracking features provided by the affiliate network or platform to measure the number of conversions and the revenue generated. This helps you assess the performance of different products or merchants you promote.

c) Reports and Metrics: Explore the various reports and metrics offered by the affiliate network or platform. These may include metrics such as clicks, impressions, conversion rates, or earnings. Analyze these reports to gain insights into the performance of your affiliate campaigns.

d) Deep Linking Analytics: If your affiliate network or platform supports deep linking, utilize the associated analytics to measure the performance of specific deep-linked pages or products. This allows you to assess the effectiveness of deep linking strategies.

3. Social Media Analytics:
If you leverage social media platforms for promoting your affiliate products, utilize their built-in analytics tools to track and measure your performance. Consider the following features and strategies:

a) Engagement Metrics: Analyze engagement metrics such as likes, comments, shares, and click-throughs on your social media posts. These metrics indicate how well your content resonates with your audience and the level of interest it generates.

b) Audience Insights: Utilize the audience insights provided by social media platforms to understand the demographics, interests, and behaviors of your followers. This helps you tailor your content and promotions to better suit your audience.

c) Referral Traffic: Track the referral traffic from social media platforms to your website or landing pages using Google Analytics or other web analytics tools. This allows you to assess the effectiveness of your social media campaigns in driving website visits and conversions.

d) A/B Testing: Experiment with different variations of your social media posts, captions, or ad creatives to identify the most engaging and high-converting content. Use social media analytics to measure the performance of each variant and make data-driven decisions.

4. URL Tracking and UTM Parameters: Implement URL tracking and utilize UTM parameters to track and measure the performance of different marketing channels, campaigns, or promotional strategies. Consider the following strategies:

a) URL Tracking: Create unique URLs for each marketing channel or campaign by appending tracking parameters. This allows you to distinguish and measure the performance of each traffic source or campaign.

b) UTM Parameters: Utilize UTM parameters to add specific tags to your URLs, indicating the source, medium, and campaign name. This enables you to track the performance of individual campaigns in Google Analytics or other analytics platforms.

c) Source Attribution: Analyze the performance of different traffic sources, such as organic search, paid search, social media, or email marketing, based on the data collected through URL tracking and UTM parameters. Adjust your marketing efforts based on the sources that drive the highest conversions and revenue.

d) Campaign Comparison: Compare the performance of different campaigns or marketing initiatives by analyzing the data collected through URL tracking. Identify the campaigns that generate the most clicks, conversions, or revenue, and optimize your strategies accordingly.

Conclusion:

Utilizing analytics tools is vital for tracking and measuring your affiliate marketing efforts. Google Analytics, affiliate network and platform analytics, social media analytics, and URL tracking with UTM parameters provide valuable insights into website performance, user behavior, campaign effectiveness, and revenue generation. By regularly monitoring and analyzing the data from these tools, you can make informed decisions, optimize your marketing strategies, and achieve better results in your affiliate marketing endeavors. Remember to set goals, track key metrics, and continuously refine your strategies based on the insights gained. With the power of analytics, you can drive success and maximize your affiliate marketing performance.

- Making data-driven decisions to optimize your campaigns and improve results.

Making data-driven decisions is crucial for optimizing your affiliate marketing campaigns and achieving improved results. By analyzing relevant data and metrics, you can gain insights into your campaign performance, identify areas for improvement, and make informed decisions to drive success. In this chapter, we will explore strategies for making data-driven decisions to optimize your campaigns and improve your affiliate marketing results.

1. Define Clear Objectives and Key Performance Indicators (KPIs):
Start by defining clear objectives for your affiliate marketing campaigns. These objectives should align with your overall business goals. Next, identify the key performance indicators (KPIs) that will help you track and measure progress towards those objectives. Common KPIs include click-through rates (CTR), conversion rates, revenue,

return on investment (ROI), and customer acquisition costs (CAC).

2. Gather and Analyze Data:
Collect relevant data from various sources such as affiliate network reports, analytics platforms, social media insights, and customer feedback. Consider the following strategies:

a) Affiliate Network Reports: Analyze reports provided by your affiliate network to track clicks, conversions, and revenue generated from your affiliate links. Identify top-performing products, merchants, and campaigns.

b) Analytics Platforms: Utilize web analytics tools such as Google Analytics to track user behavior, traffic sources, and on-site conversions. Analyze data related to bounce rates, session duration, and goal completions to gain insights into user engagement and campaign effectiveness.

c) Social Media Insights: Monitor social media analytics to understand the performance of your social media campaigns. Analyze engagement metrics, reach, and audience demographics to refine your targeting and content strategies.

d) Customer Feedback: Gather feedback from your audience through surveys, reviews, or direct communication channels. Understand their preferences, pain points, and expectations to align your campaigns with their needs.

3. Conduct A/B Testing:
A/B testing involves comparing different variations of your campaigns to identify the most effective elements. Split your audience into two or more groups and test one variable at a time, such as different headlines, images, call-to-actions, or landing page layouts. Analyze the results to determine which variations perform better and drive higher conversions. Use this data to optimize your campaigns and make data-driven decisions about the elements that resonate most with your audience.

4. Monitor and Optimize Conversion Funnels:
Analyze your conversion funnels to identify potential bottlenecks or areas for improvement.

A conversion funnel represents the journey a visitor takes from initial contact to final conversion. By monitoring each stage of the funnel and analyzing drop-off points, you can optimize the user experience and make data-driven decisions to enhance conversions. Optimize landing pages, simplify checkout processes, or provide additional support to overcome barriers and improve overall conversion rates.

5. Implement Personalization and Segmentation:
Segment your audience based on demographics, behavior, or preferences to deliver more personalized experiences and targeted campaigns. Analyze the performance of each segment to identify their specific needs, interests, and pain points. Use this data to tailor your messaging, content, and offers to resonate with each segment individually. Personalization and segmentation allow you to make data-driven decisions about how to best engage and convert different audience segments.

6. Regularly Review and Adjust:

Regularly review your data and metrics to track progress and identify trends. Analyze your campaigns' performance over time to identify patterns and seasonal variations. Compare the performance of different campaigns, channels, or promotional strategies to determine what works best for your audience. Based on your analysis, make data-driven decisions to adjust your campaigns, optimize your strategies, and allocate resources effectively.

7. Stay Informed and Embrace New Technologies:

Stay up to date with industry trends, emerging technologies, and best practices in affiliate marketing. Attend conferences, webinars, or networking events to learn from industry experts. Embrace new tools, automation technologies, or tracking capabilities that can further enhance your data-driven decision-making process. Continuously educate yourself and adapt your strategies based on advancements in the field.

Conclusion:

Making data-driven decisions is essential for optimizing your affiliate marketing campaigns and improving your results. By defining clear objectives, gathering and analyzing relevant data, conducting A/B testing, monitoring conversion funnels, implementing personalization and segmentation, and regularly reviewing and adjusting your strategies, you can make informed decisions that lead to campaign optimization and improved outcomes. Embrace the power of data, leverage analytics tools, and stay informed about industry trends to continuously refine and optimize your affiliate marketing efforts. With a data-driven approach, you can drive success and maximize the performance of your campaigns.

Congratulations on the completion of your Affiliate Marketing Mastery ebook! This remarkable achievement signifies your commitment to acquiring the knowledge and strategies necessary to thrive in the ever-evolving world of affiliate marketing. By arming yourself with the insights contained within this guide, you are well-prepared to embark on a journey towards generating passive income online through affiliate marketing.

It's important to recognize that success in this field is not an overnight accomplishment, but rather a result of continuous learning, adaptability, and perseverance. As you implement the strategies and tactics outlined in your ebook, remember to remain open to new ideas and stay informed about the latest trends and developments in the industry. Affiliate marketing is a dynamic and evolving landscape, and staying ahead of the curve will be instrumental in your long-term success.

While your ebook provides valuable information and guidance, it is crucial to address the legal aspects to ensure you are fully protected. Please note that the following disclaimer should be included to protect both yourself as the author and the readers:

"Disclaimer: The information provided in this ebook is for informational purposes only. The author and publisher are not engaged in rendering legal, financial, or professional advice. The content of this ebook should not be relied upon as a substitute for professional advice. The author and publisher disclaim any liability for any actions taken by the readers based on the information provided. Results may vary, and success in affiliate marketing depends on individual effort, dedication, and market conditions. Readers are advised to conduct their own research and seek the advice of professionals before making any business or financial decisions."

By incorporating this comprehensive disclaimer, you ensure that readers understand the limitations of the information provided and take responsibility for their own actions. It sets clear expectations and safeguards both parties involved.

As you continue your journey in affiliate marketing, remember that your success hinges on your ability to adapt, learn, and persevere. Stay curious, explore new opportunities, and embrace the challenges that come your way. Your determination combined with the knowledge gained from your ebook will undoubtedly propel you towards a fulfilling and prosperous career in affiliate marketing.

Wishing you great success and fulfillment as you venture into the world of affiliate marketing and generate passive income online!

- Nicholas Davis